CATCHING
HELL

CATCHING HELL

THE INSIDER STORY OF SEAFOOD FROM OCEAN TO PLATE

ALLEN RICCA AND JOE MUTO

Skyhorse Publishing

Skyhorse Publishing books may be purchased in bulk at special discounts for sales promotion, corporate gifts, fund-raising, or educational purposes. Special editions can also be created to specifications. For details, contact the Special Sales Department, Skyhorse Publishing, 307 West 36th Street, 11th Floor, New York, NY 10018 or info@skyhorsepublishing.com.

Skyhorse® and Skyhorse Publishing® are registered trademarks of Skyhorse Publishing, Inc.®, a Delaware corporation.

Visit our website at www.skyhorsepublishing.com.

10 9 8 7 6 5 4 3 2 1

Library of Congress Cataloging-in-Publication Data is available on file.

Cover design by Brian Peterson
Cover image by Getty Images

Print ISBN: 978-1-5107-6970-0
Ebook ISBN: 978-1-5107-6971-7

Printed in the United States of America

For Caylin
—AR

For Max
—JM

CONTENTS

PROLOGUE
Yeezy & Me

THE MOOD IN the dining room that night was electric.

And that was *before* Kanye showed up.

So when the famously eccentric millionaire rapper appeared at the hostess stand with a small entourage (but *without* his reality star wife), the vibe quickly went from electric to absolutely crackling.

This was a few years back: pre-COVID, so the restaurant was jammed, with every tightly packed table full; it was also well before West's bizarre flirtation with Trumpism, so the hip downtown Manhattan diners were, at the time, actually pretty happy to see him.

Not that any of them showed obvious signs of excitement, of course. They were way too cool for that. There was some nudging and murmuring, and a noticeable uptick in people subtly pulling out their phones taking selfies, angled *just-so*, to make sure the hip-hop legend would appear in the background. But no one did anything embarrassing like jump up and ask for an autograph. (Even if they had, the entourage's hulking security guard, who appeared to possess both the size and demeanor of an NFL nose tackle, probably would have intercepted them.)

I caught the eye of the manager as he marched toward my table, on his way to the front to greet the VIP. I'd known him a while, and he was a pro. A celeb wasn't going to ruffle his feathers one bit. This establishment was the type of perennial hot spot that had a fairly steady rotation of famous clientele, counting people like Jon Bon Jovi, Heidi

Klum, Kelly Ripa, and Sarah Jessica Parker as regulars. He smiled at me and shook his head slightly as he whisked past. *Can you believe this shit?*

Just another day on the job for him.

After Kanye and his entourage were ushered to a banquette in the back corner of the restaurant and settled in, the dining room calmed down a little. People still craned their necks periodically to catch a glimpse, but there wasn't much to see at this point. Just a very rich guy and his friends ordering bottles of champagne and mountains of shell-fish and sushi rolls.

Now I'm not going to pretend that I'm completely immune to the charms of celebrity. I admit I snuck a glance or two myself. But that night I was actually much more interested in the food that was going to his table.

Because I knew that a good chunk of what the restaurant was serving was absolute shit.

And I knew this because I was the one who had given it to them.

My name is Allen Ricca. I sell fish.

And not just any fish—the best goddamn seafood on the Eastern Seaboard of the United States, if not the entire country. But that quality, as you can imagine, comes at a price. Many of my customers are willing to pay that price, because they're passing the cost onto *their* customers anyway, at a healthy two-or three-fold markup.

But this restaurant—this celeb-magnet, gossip-page-fixture in the most fashionable neighborhood in New York City—wasn't content to take that reasonable profit margin.

No, they didn't want to make back two or three times their money. They were greedy. They wanted ten to twenty.

Let me give you an example. One of the products I'd been supplying to this restaurant is shrimp. When they first started buying from me, they were still establishing their relationship, and they only wanted the best stuff: beautiful wild-caught shrimp, shipped in from the sparkling waters off the coast of Mexico. They paid me a pretty penny for it, but of course then they turned around and put it on the menu for an even prettier penny: like $25 for a 5-piece shrimp cocktail, or $8 for a single sushi *nigiri*.

This restaurant built their reputation on my shrimp and the other high-quality products they were serving. But once they'd established their culinary cred and cultivated their ultra-cool, well-heeled clientele, they turned on a dime. They didn't want the best stuff anymore.

They only wanted the cheapest.

No more wild shrimp from Mexico. They started asking instead for the farmed shrimp from India.

I mean, this shrimp is edible, sure. It's not going to kill you or anything. (After all, I'm not in the business of poisoning people.) But it certainly isn't what I would consider *good*. It's bland. Virtually tasteless. The only reason I even keep it in stock is that it's insanely popular with a lot of my customers that own Chinese takeouts. You know these places if you've ever been to New York, where they line every avenue: small storefronts with an ordering window, maybe a table or two. Definitely no celebs filling those tables.

Anyway, I sell the farmed Indian shrimp to these takeout restaurants for 30 to 40 cents per shrimp. And don't get me wrong—it's plenty tasty in a kung pao, or battered, deep-fried, and smothered with bright red sweet and sour sauce. (In those cases, its relative blandness is actually a virtue, allowing it to play nice with all those other strong flavors.) So while it's not bad, it's definitely not something you'd expect to get served at a high-end restaurant, especially when you, the customer, are on the hook for something like $5 to $8 per shrimp.

That sudden decline in the quality of their purchases was the reason I was even at the restaurant the night that Kanye showed up. I was there to plead with the chef to switch back to the good stuff. This was for business reasons, of course—naturally, I'd rather sell them the high-end, high-profit product! But I was also there to appeal to the chef's sense of culinary pride. He wanted to present his food as "the best," I argued, when he was clearly serving something that was very much not that.

My pleas fell on deaf ears, unfortunately. The chef explained that he was under immense pressure from the owners to keep costs down. They weren't food guys: rather, they were hedge fund and finance types who wanted to wring every last penny out of their "dining concept."

That's what it was to them—not a restaurant, just a franchise opportunity.

They'd recently leveraged the jolt of popularity that their Manhattan location was currently experiencing to secure financing for other locations: Miami, Vegas, Dallas, Dubai, and so on. They had big plans to open outlets in various locales where there was a lot of money floating around in the hands of a lot of people who weren't particularly discerning about what they spent it on, as long as it seemed cool and exclusive.

The chef led me through the kitchen as we chatted, where a small army of line cooks were prepping for that night's dinner service. We went into the walk-in cooler and freezer where I immediately clocked a case of my Chinese-takeout shrimp, sitting next to boxes of product that *definitely* hadn't come from me.

When I started selling to these guys, they'd wanted the best of the best for everything. Not just the wild Mexican shrimp, but also squid from Rhode Island, giant lobster tails from South Africa, and of course Alaskan-caught Red King Crab. Now that I read the labels on the boxes I realized with horror that the cheaper shrimp from me was the least of their problems. They had found some truly unscrupulous supplier to sell them some of the worst seafood on the planet. Brown king crab from Russia, frozen into shards that I could tell were more ice than crab; pre-cut squid rings and tentacles from China; lobster tails from God-knows-where.

The horror on my face must have shown, because the chef immediately paused his chatter, and shrugged with resignation.

"Yup. This is how it is now," he said with a sigh. He ruefully looked over the sub-par contents of the walk-in, shaking his head.

"Anyway, Allen . . . you want to stay for dinner?"

IT WAS LATER that night, as I sat in the dining room, that the germ of an idea for this book started to form. There I was, at my table as the model-beautiful servers buzzed around me; the music was pumping; the tasteful lighting was emanating from the crystal chandeliers overhead; the cocktails were flowing. I was surrounded by the rich, fabulous, and famous—and they were unknowingly getting fleeced with every bite they took.

Not that most of you are going to shed any tears for some Wall Street bros who drop $300 per person on a meal as easily as the rest of us buy a Big Mac (ironically, McDonald's would have been a tastier dining experience than this restaurant). I'm not writing this book for those guys, though.

I'm writing this book for the honest guy who maybe saved up his cash for a few weeks or a few months to take his wife somewhere nice. Doesn't he deserve to get his money's worth?

I'm writing this book for the skilled chefs and restaurateurs who put their heart and soul into their establishments, and never cut corners even when it would benefit them financially. Someone needs to be their champion.

I'm writing this book for my hardworking employees—many of them young, many of them immigrants or children of immigrants—who are just as passionate about this business as I am, and who deserve to see the sweat and labor they put into it respected and celebrated.

And most of all, dear reader, I'm writing this book for *you.*

Because this is a hell of a good story, and I'm going to have a hell of a good time telling it.

Chapter 1
THE BIG CON

I LOVE THE seafood business.

Which is why it pains me so much to admit that lying, cheating, fraud, and outright theft are embedded into its very DNA.

There are some good actors out there, of course. I'd like to think that I'm one. I try to do things the right way. But that honesty comes at a price. I'm losing business every day to people who have no qualms about grifting everyone they come into contact with: their clients, their suppliers, their employees, and (I can only assume) their wives, their children, and probably even their pets.

That's what I'm up against—guys who will scam their *own fucking dogs*.

All this bad behavior might not seem like it's a problem to you, the humble diner, but it has a way of trickling down. If I lose business to an unscrupulous competitor selling crap product, then I have two options: one, I can try to beat him at his own game, selling equally bad food even cheaper than him. That, of course, will trigger a race to the bottom and everyone will suffer. I definitely don't want to take that route. But then my second option if I start losing money to the competitors and their inferior wares, is that I have to boost my prices on my high-quality product to make up the difference. The restaurant will go on to pass those charges onto the customer as much as they can, but that leads to their margins getting smaller, and they'll be forced to make up the difference in other ways. Maybe they skimp on portion sizes. Maybe they water down the drinks. Maybe they start stocking the bathrooms with single ply. You get the point.

In other words, all it takes is a single bad actor to set off a butterfly effect leading to you, the next time you're at a restaurant, overpaying. You're either overpaying for the good product or —even worse—overpaying for the bad one.

This has to stop.

It's why I wrote this book. I'm not pulling any punches here. I'm pointing fingers, I'm naming names. Distributors, restaurateurs, chefs, critics—every facet of this business we all love is due for a reckoning. I'm sparing no one.

Not even myself.

Because make no mistake: my side of the business deserves a lot of the blame.

HERE'S A FEW of the ways people on my end are looking to get one over on you:

First, substitutions—this is one of the oldest, most common scams. In an industry with as many products as ours, there are too many opportunities to slip things past people who know less than you do.

Take, for example, "Dayboat" scallops. In theory, they're great. Dayboat means that they're not coming from a fishing vessel that's been out to sea for weeks. It means they're fresh from a boat that went out that morning and came back that night.

In theory.

In practice, of course, unscrupulous distributors will slap a "Dayboat" label on anything they think they can get away with. That could be "Overnight" scallops, which are less fresh and often soaked in a water-based solution designed to plump them up. Or that could even be frozen scallops, plucked from the sea weeks or months ago, and defrosted just in time to be pawned off on a restaurant kitchen that doesn't know any better.

I can tell the difference between these types. Any chef worth his salt can tell the difference too. But can buyers—who are often juggling dozens of suppliers—tell the difference? Will they even check? And if they do figure it out, will they even know the value differential, so they can tell how badly they're getting hosed?

It depends on the buyer. It depends on the restaurant. But chances are, they won't know any of those things. They'll take the seller's word for it.

That's what the scammers are banking on. That no one will check. And that even if someone does check, they won't have the know-how to detect the scam in the first place. Or they won't have the confidence to call out the distributor. It's not necessarily even the restaurant's fault, at that point. But it's definitely the person eating there who's paying the price for it.

Another way that sellers get one over on restaurants: let's call it "The Name Game."

A restaurant will often place an order for "white shrimp." That's an industry term. It's also an extremely vague one. A white shrimp is an umbrella name for dozens of different kinds of shrimp. A white shrimp could be farmed or wild. It could be from America, or Asia, or Central America or South America or India. It could be one of a half-dozen different size categories.

Depending on the specific combination of all of these options, we're potentially talking a price swing of plus or minus $5 a pound.

But a lot of restaurants don't take that into account. They just ask for "white shrimp." No specifics beyond that.

At this point, the restaurant has essentially given the distributor permission to fuck with their menu. The menu promises one thing—shrimp from the Gulf of Mexico. The distributor delivers another—shrimp from Thailand or the Indian Ocean. The restaurant has put their trust in the distributor, and now they're in the position of inadvertently lying to all their customers, not realizing that their system of receiving their product is fundamentally broken.

When a lot of distributors hear a restaurant order "white shrimp," they see it as an opportunity to unload whatever junk they have sitting in the back of the chill chest. The restaurant is going to get the cheapest possible product that can still technically be called that name. If the restaurant presses the distributor on it, the distributor can always say, "Well, you asked for white shrimp, and that's what we gave you." And the distributor wouldn't be wrong.

They'd be a dick, but they wouldn't be wrong.

It's the equivalent of walking into a Best Buy and saying "Give me a flatscreen TV." The employee brings you a 32-inch from a no-name brand and says, "That'll be $2,000 please."

"But I was expecting a 75-inch Samsung!" you might protest.

"You didn't say that, though," the employee replies. "You just said you wanted a flatscreen TV. So here you go."

Of course, the main difference here is that it's pretty easy to tell televisions apart. You just look for the manufacturer's label, or consult the thousands of websites who do research and keep tabs on that sort of thing.

There's no such informational backstop for seafood. Salmon fillets don't come stamped with little brand names. The people who catch and pack your squid aren't going to show up on a Google search. Oftentimes it's literally impossible to judge by appearance alone. The difference in quality only reveals itself when it's on the diners' plates, and by then it's too late.

HERE'S YET ANOTHER grift: the confusion around weighing.

Some seafood sellers will offer to break down whole fish into fillets for the restaurant. This is a great service. It saves the kitchen valuable prep time. But the hidden downside is that oftentimes the restaurant has no idea what they paid for.

Say a whole fish weighs in at about twenty pounds. A distributor tells a restaurant they can give them the fish for about $4.25 a pound, and they'll cut it into fillets for them. But a fish, of course, isn't entirely fillets. A fish is also skin, scales, bones, head, and tail. Subtract all that, and out of a twenty-pound fish, you might be looking at only ten or eleven pounds of actual edible product.

But the restaurant, meanwhile, *thinks* it got twenty pounds. After all, when they got the invoice, it *said* twenty pounds.

Then when I, another distributor, come in a week later, and tell them my price for fillets is $7.75 a pound, they hem and haw and complain that so-and-so gave them the same fish for more than $3 a pound less. I have to explain to them that when we sell them the fillet, we *price in* all the waste and all the labor that's involved with producing that fillet. It looks more expensive on paper, but in reality, they're paying less per pound of actual usable food.

Here's the kicker—half the time they don't believe me!

"No," they'll insist, "I got twenty pounds of fillets for $4.25 a pound. I have the receipt!" I've gone so far as to break out a scale in front of them and weighed their "twenty pounds" of fillets. They are completely blown away—shocked—when the scale registers barely half that.

AT THIS POINT you might be thinking there's no hope. That this is an irredeemable industry, filled with liars, cheats, and corner-cutters.

And truth be told, some days even I think that!

But I reassure myself with the knowledge that there's a small but potent contingent of people who do it the right way. As satisfying and cathartic as it would be to spend the next couple hundred of pages doing nothing but pointing out what's wrong with the industry, I feel compelled to also use this book to celebrate what's actually working well, and to single out those people and organizations who are doing the right things.

If there's one thing I've learned that I can pass along to you, the restaurant-going public, it's that you should seek out mom-and-pop establishments wherever you can find them. Maybe I'm a little biased because I'm also a part of a multi-generational family business, but there's something about these restaurants that puts them a cut above. In New York City, you'll most often find them in outer boroughs. Or elsewhere in the country, they won't be in the hippest neighborhoods. They might be in areas that have their best days behind them. They won't be serving the most modern cuisine. A lot of them will be red-sauce Italian joints. But the thing they have in common?

The food is spectacular.

I'm talking about someone like my friend Joe, who runs Marco Polo Ristorante in Carroll Gardens, Brooklyn. He cares so much about the quality of his fish that it almost drives me crazy sometimes. But I'd much rather have a customer who cares too much—who is *too* meticulous, and *too* knowledgeable—than the opposite. The amazing thing is that Joe seems to have passed his keen buyer's eye onto his son Marco. So I look forward to doing business with them and their great restaurant for decades to come.

(For those of you who get a chance to visit that neighborhood, just a few blocks away is another father-son operation, a little retail market called Fish Tales. It's run by Chris and his dad John, and they never ask me to bring them anything but the best I have to offer.)

The list of small, family restaurateurs who care deeply about their product goes on and on. There's Michael at the famous Don Peppe near JFK Airport. Not only do they have the best baked clams you'll ever put in your piehole, but they are the most discerning purchasers of scungilli (that's conch, for you non-*Paisans*) I've ever had the pleasure to come across. Or Tony from Park Side in Corona, Queens, who has a bread course so good that it could serve as a full meal in and of itself, but who also fusses over every piece of jumbo wild shrimp I sell him like a mother taking care of their infant.

There's Sammy of Sammy's Fish Box, Sammy's Shrimp Box, and Sammy's Sea Shore, a budding empire of restaurants on City Island in the Bronx. This guy is obsessed with putting the absolute best product on plates: South African lobster tails, wild shrimp from all over, beautiful red king crab, snow crab, and so on. No matter how high the price, he *must* have the product! If there were any justice in the world, Sammy would have all the Michelin stars he wanted and celebrity chefs would be calling every night begging for reservations.

These mom-and-pop restaurants are, from my standpoint as a supplier, usually the most difficult to please. But if I had my way I'd want every restaurant in the city to follow their lead. These aren't the coolest places. They're not trendy. They're not going to have celebrities dropping in on a regular basis. (Though some of you might remember a few years back Don Peppe factored heavily into a plot line on the HBO show *Entourage*.) What they are is down-to-earth, honest establishments with exacting standards. Yes, they're demanding, but in my mind that just means they care about their customers. They want to give diners exactly what they're paying for.

That said, I still appreciate it when I see some of the big boys who are doing it well. Take someone like ONE Hospitality, which owns the chains STK Steakhouse and Kona Grill. They bill themselves as "Leaders in Vibe Dining," but don't hold that awkward tagline against them; they use some of the highest-end products you'll ever see and never balk at continuing to purchase top-of-the-line seafood even when the price goes up.

Or Limani, a high-end Mediterranean chain with locations in midtown Manhattan and Roslyn, New York. They care about their products and never take shortcuts, even when a lot of their fellow white-tablecloth establishments are tempted to do so.

Some of the big operators that are doing it right might even surprise you. Take, for instance, the Wetanson family, which owns New York City's ubiquitous, moderately-priced chain Dallas BBQ, as well as Times Square mainstay Tony's DiNapoli. One could excuse them for shrugging and making the argument that their customers aren't paying as much, and have lower expectations, but that doesn't stop the family from serving only the best domestic squid and wild shrimp at Tony's.

THIS BOOK WAS a long time coming. I've been talking about it for a while, running the idea past my friends, family, employees, and customers. And they've all asked me why I wanted to write it.

"You have a nice life, Allen," they'll say. "You have a nice business. Why rock the boat? Why risk poking people in the eye?"

I always answer that it's not about settling scores. It's not about tooting my own horn.

It's about you.

That's right; I'm doing it for you, the reader.

I want you to become better consumers. To understand seafood better. You should know exactly what you're ordering at restaurants. You should know what you're buying at the grocery store or the fish market.

I want to teach you which products you should always be wary of, and which ones are the safest bets with the highest degree of success.

Seafood can be hard to access. Mysterious. Scary, even. It's part of what makes it so desirable. But it can also make it intimidating for someone who is new to it, or who doesn't get to sample it all that much.

I can't tell you how many evening and weekend phone calls and texts I field from friends, panicked, who just sat down at a new restaurant, opened the menu, and realized they were completely lost.

"Allen, what should I order here?"

"Allen, is sea bass any good?"

"Allen, what the hell is this thing they just put in front of me?"

My goal is that this book becomes the literary equivalent of having me on speed dial. By the time you finish reading, you should have a baseline of knowledge that will empower you to confidently navigate any seafood-forward menu at any restaurant in the world.

So let's get started.

Chapter 2

WHO THE HELL AM I AND WHY ARE YOU LISTENING TO ME?

NEW YORK CITY in the late 1970s was a wonderland of disco music, cocaine, big night clubs, and even bigger lapels. It was very glamorous, I'm told—unless you were spending all your time in Chinatown at a seafood distribution company on Elizabeth Street, which is exactly what my father was doing.

Vallie "Val" Ricca wasn't impressed by the Studio 54 crowd. He'd grown up dirt poor— one of his oft-repeated (hilarious, possibly exaggerated) stories involves sitting down to dinner with his family and being forced to share a single napkin—and he had always been focused on hard work instead of leisure. He didn't have time to do The Hustle; he was too busy hustling for every penny.

My father was always looking for ways to make money even as a kid: collecting bottles or cans from the trash, or selling newspapers to the guys laying railroad tracks near his Staten Island home. He had a preternatural knack for business, and a penchant for saving instead of spending. "Anyone can make money," went the refrain he'd drill into me later. "The hard part is keeping it."

After high school he dabbled in the hippie lifestyle and was a nomad for a few years. He hiked the Appalachian Trail; did a stint in Jamaica building homes for charity; went to Europe with his buddy Barry and spent several months as a ski bum in the Austrian Alps. When he did finally settle back in NYC, he got really into jazz, satisfying his habit by sneaking into shows at Carnegie Hall and the Village Vanguard.

But being a hippie can only get you so far, even in the low-rent parts of seventies Manhattan, so he had to get honest work, or at least semi-honest. That's how he ended up on Elizabeth Street, a 6'2" Italian painfully conspicuous next to the rest of the mostly-immigrant-Chinese workforce. But he was a hard worker, and endlessly affable, so he had no trouble getting quickly accepted by his coworkers as one of their own.

Fishmongers keep weird hours, and my father embraced this life-style, unloading crates or visiting the Fulton Fish Market in the wee morning hours. He loved staying up late playing cards with the gang, especially when the stakes were high: the losers had to pick up the whole tab for the group for the sumptuous late night "banquet" meals they'd feast on after the cards were done.

The times were good, but they didn't last that long. The owner didn't have much of a head for business, but he did have an insatiable desire for the finer things in life. The combination turned out to be a recipe for disaster. While revenue was decent, any money coming in went immediately to the owner's multiple apartments, rotating cast of girlfriends, jewelry, fur coats, a Rolls Royce and—not uncommon for the late seventies—Scarface-style mountains of blow.

"He basically put the company up his nose," my dad told me. The whole operation went belly-up like a dead carp, leaving the employees scrambling.

Luckily, by then, my dad knew the ropes. As a salesman, he'd got-ten a close look at the way the business was run. He understood the cash flow. He had established relationships with restaurants around the city, knew what products they liked, and how best to sell them those products.

He'd never run his own business before, but after watching his old boss for a while, he was pretty sure he at least knew what *not* to do (cocaine, for starters).

So he bought a truck and set out on his own.

Val's Ocean Pacific was started in 1982. Just in time, too, because my father was no longer making a living only for himself.

WHILE VAL WAS growing up poor in Staten Island, across the Verrazano Bridge in Brooklyn my mother was growing up not much more well off. Janet Allison Murray, whose initials led to the affectionate nickname of "Jam" that would follow her throughout her life, became a schoolteacher.

Early in her career, she went on a ski trip with some work friends. It was a big group of twenty-somethings renting a small house, with everyone just bunking wherever they could find some floor space, as people in that stage of their life tend to do. My mother didn't know everyone in the house, so she was on her best behavior, but after one night in the common sleeping room she had a beef that she felt needed airing in front of the entire group, strangers-be-damned.

"Who was that snoring all night?" she asked over breakfast. "I barely slept it was so loud!" After some murmuring amongst the group, a tall, shaggy-haired hippieish-looking guy raised his hand with a grin.

"Sorry about that," said Val Ricca. And that was their first meeting.

They were both dating other people at the time, but when you meet your soulmate, your current relationship is apparently just a formality. A few weeks later both were single. Then they started dating, and the rest is history.

One of my mom's favorite stories from my father's courtship of her involves the first time she met his family on Staten Island. Jam didn't come from that much of a foodie family, so it was a bit of a culture shock for her to meet my old-school Italian grandmother who was a world-class cook and a true eccentric in the best way possible. The woman was cooking constantly, staying up til 3:00 a.m. sometimes baking, or making fresh pasta.

Remember that scene from *Goodfellas*, when they visit Joe Pesci's mother's house in the middle of the night after killing a fellow gangster, and she insists on cooking them a full meal? That's basically my grandma! (Of course, my dad and his friends weren't coming home late from a night of murdering. Mostly, I gather, they just went to concerts, where the only thing they'd kill was a joint or two.)

Anyway, that first night it was my mom at my dad's childhood home. She wants to be helpful in the kitchen, so she offers to assist my grandma in preparing the dinner. My grandma asks her to grab something from the fridge, and when Jam opens it up she barely stops herself from screaming. There, on the top shelf of the fridge, casually sitting on a plate, is *the severed head of a fully-grown goat.*

My mother to this day says she can barely remember the rest of the night because she was so in shock that she almost passed out.

But even the goat incident couldn't derail my parents' love for each other, and they were soon married. I was welcomed as the older of the two children; my sister Emily would follow shortly thereafter.

This was about the time that my dad found himself unemployed after his coke-hoovering boss tanked the company. He had two little kids and a wife (who was employed, thankfully, but not exactly making big bucks working for the NYC public school system) to think of. But my father was nothing if not confident in himself. He decided to roll the dice.

His gamble paid off almost immediately. He started with a single truck. By the time I was old enough to remember anything, he was hiring his first bookkeeper, along with two additional truck drivers. When I was entering kindergarten, he ditched the warehouse space he'd been renting from a larger company and bought his own building. By the time I was in third grade, he'd expanded his employees to include salesmen and purchasers, and he suddenly realized that in less than a decade he'd built a company that was already larger and more successful than the one he used to work for.

I'VE TOLD YOU about my grandma, so with that blood running through my veins it will come as no surprise to you that my upbringing was centered around food.

Oddly enough, I started life as a picky eater. Naturally, it was Grandma Ricca who quickly nipped that one in the bud. When I was barely a year old, my parents were headed out of town for a weekend and left me with Grandma Ricca. My folks were a little nervous about the whole thing, mainly on account of me being a terrible eater. I rejected almost everything that was put in front of me, and they were worried I'd go hungry the entire weekend.

Before they left, they tried to dictate to my grandma the very short list of things that I actually would eat, but she tut-tutted them out the door and told them she'd be fine. They reluctantly went.

When they came back a few days later, they asked how I'd eaten.

"No problem," my grandma said. "He was eating the whole weekend. No issues at all." They were stunned. How'd she get Allen to eat?

So she showed them. She grabbed a piece of pasta with tomato sauce with one hand, and used her other hand to pinch my nose, causing my mouth to droop open. Then she shoved in the food, and closed my mouth for me, working my jaw up and down, essentially doing the chewing for me.

I was never picky about food again after that day, so I'm told.

Now, as an adult, all my favorite memories as a kid are food-based. Like the marathon dim sum sessions in Chinatown my family did almost every weekend. My father liked to order a whole steamed fish for the table, but always insisted that the waiters step aside so he himself could do the honors of cutting off the head and dividing it into fillets. This was very much against Chinese tradition, which dictated that the person bringing the fish to the table be the one to carve it, but we were regular enough customers that the staff at the dim sum place let him have his way. (Also against tradition: instead of tea with our meal we always drank Minute Maid Orange Soda. I don't know why that became our drink of choice, but I can tell you that to this day any time I catch so much as a whiff of that synthetic orange flavor my mouth starts watering for dumplings.)

My parents brought me and my sister up to be tiny culinary warriors. Manhattan was not quite as family-friendly in the eighties as it is today, but they still made a point of hauling us everywhere, taking a decidedly laid-back attitude to things like "bedtimes." We were still both toddlers the time they brought us to dinner at the Four Seasons, for example. But we were well-behaved, dammit. Even at a young age, we knew how to eat at a nice restaurant, even if that meant we both fell asleep at the table well before the entrees came.

Another family tradition that some may find gauche but I wholeheartedly believe makes total sense is that if we were ever invited to a wedding we'd always make sure to go out to a restaurant for a good meal, *before* the reception. That meant sometimes sneaking out of the church a few minutes early and cramming in a 4:30 p.m. dinner before hitting the wedding's cocktail hour at 6:00 p.m., but it at least ensured that we'd never be forced to suffer through the rubber chicken and overcooked salmon that are sadly too common at these happy occasions.

Since it was skiing that brought my parents together in the first place, one of the first things they invested in after Val's Ocean Pacific started doing pretty well was a house in Vermont. It wasn't large, it wasn't fancy, but it was on five lovely secluded acres, and it was a short drive to some of the best slopes on the Eastern Seaboard.

In true Ricca family style, we even structured our drives to the ski house around meals. Believe it or not, one of the most authentic, delicious Japanese restaurants in the entire country was northeast of Albany, New York, just after you crossed the border into Vermont—a surprising, out-of-the-way location that made it one of the best-kept secrets of the culinary world. We'd always time our departures with an eye toward hitting that part of the journey right around dinner time. The fine people at Yoshi came to expect us every few weeks, and it got to the point where we barely even needed to tell them what we wanted to order. They'd just present us with a beautiful spread of sushi soon after we walked through the door.

It wasn't all about restaurants for us, of course. My dad had inherited his mother's penchant for cooking, and my mother was no slouch herself, so they kept us fueled with hearty fare during those cold Vermont weekends. We'd always start the day with creamed chipped beef on English muffins. It sure didn't look like much—the old military nickname for the dish was "shit on a shingle," my dad loved to point out—but it was warm and filling and kept you going on the slopes all day. For a late lunch/early dinner we'd have steaming homemade chili, loaded up with cheese and sour cream, served in bread bowls (chili being yet another entry in the "looks bad, tastes amazing" school of cuisine).

In the summers we'd pick blueberries til our fingers were stained purple, carting home bushels to eat over cereal, or bake into muffins. Any leftovers, my mother would use to make preserves. We kids would sell jars on the side of the road—Jam's Jam, our handwritten sign would say.

On the way home from these weekends we'd sneak in one last culinary delight—stopping at gas stations to pick up bags of potato chips, *oohing and aaahing* over all the strange, exotic brands and flavors that you couldn't get in New York.

When you're a kid, the Four Seasons is fine, but nothing is more exciting than a bag of chips you've never tasted before.

Other kids wanted to be firemen, or policemen, or astronauts, or baseball players, but I never even considered any of these occupations. As far back as I can recall I'd tell anyone who would listen that when I grew up I wanted to be just like my dad.

I wanted to do exactly what he did.

God knows why I was drawn to it. It wasn't a particularly glamorous lifestyle he led. He worked like a dog, day and night. The hours were crappy. My dad tried his best to be present and attentive to his family, but there were plenty of nights when he was absent from the dinner table, dealing with one problem or another at work. We weren't mad about it, though. Frankly, we were all in awe of him and his work ethic. We knew and accepted that it was stressful work running a business, especially in a city as cutthroat as New York, in an industry filled with guys who wanted nothing more than to pull one over on you. Watching him navigate these treacherous waters, I always felt like we were truly witnessing greatness.

I know what you're all thinking at this point—that I just waltzed in as the boss's son and had it easy.

Honestly, that's sort of what I was thinking might happen, but I should have known better. That wasn't something Val was about to let happen.

I started working at the family business at age twenty-two. But there wasn't a corner office awaiting me on my first day of work. The red carpet was not rolled out for the heir apparent.

"What am I doing today?" I asked my father.

"Get your ass down to the loading dock," he told me.

Even though I had a college education under my belt, he was insistent that I get an entirely different type of education before I got within sniffing distance of managing the company that he thought of as his third child.

So I spent my days on the warehouse floor, loading and unloading trucks at the ass-crack of dawn. My alarm went off every day at 3:26 a.m. (I'd meant to set it for 3:25, but screwed up the first time I did it and never fixed it) and I dragged myself out of bed with just enough time to shower, grab a coffee, and hop on the six train to the Bronx, arriving just before 5:30 a.m. when the first shipments of the day hit the floor.

This schedule was not particularly accommodating to the lifestyle of a recent college grad trying to enjoy all that Manhattan's Upper East Side had to offer. There was more than one occasion when the 3:26 a.m. alarm on my phone went off, and instead of being safe in bed I was still on a stool at my local haunt, Dorrian's.

Let me tell you, those were some rough mornings at work.

But no matter how brutal my hangover was, I was always there on time. Punctuality matters.

AFTER EXPECTING A hero's welcome as the boss's kid, I have to admit that it took the wind out of my sails a little to have to start in the warehouse. I hadn't been expecting that. I obviously didn't think I'd strut in and be in charge right off the bat, but I figured I could at least have a crack at a salesman position.

My dad was insistent, though: "You're in the warehouse until I tell you you're not."

As time went on, I realized that my old man knew exactly what he was doing when he put me there. If I was going to take over the business one day, he wanted me to know it from top to bottom. And there's no better way to learn about a company top to bottom than to actually start at what was, essentially, the bottom.

My stint in a warehouse had another purpose, too, one that only dawned on me years later.

It was a test.

Chapter 3
ALLEN TAKES OVER

THE WAREHOUSE WAS a mess, and my father knew it.

It wasn't his fault, really. He was then—and still is—the most talented salesperson I know. He built the entire business to be sales-focused. And under his guidance, the company kept growing steadily for twenty-five years.

But all that sales focus meant that the biggest decision-makers at the company were siloed in the sales department, somewhat removed from the warehouse, and not aware of the chaos that was the daily order of business there. The constant growth over the years meant that the logistics team was always playing catch-up, trying to scale their operation on the fly and build an efficient system while the ground was constantly shifting under their feet.

The warehouse struggled to keep up with the massive amount of product that came in from our suppliers and went out to our customers. They were somehow making it work, day-to-day, but that was only through the herculean efforts of some pretty incredible longtime employees.

These guys needed relief. They were hanging on by their fingernails. The struggle had been going on for years, and it was only a matter of time until the rubber band finally snapped.

They needed some fresh eyes to look at their processes and diagnose what was going wrong.

They needed—apparently—me.

So that's why Val started me in the warehouse. My "graduation present," as it were, was that I was now in charge of figuring out how to fix things. It was a baptism by fire—throw the boy headfirst into the most chaotic part of the business, and see if he sinks or swims.

My father could have attempted to fix it himself, of course. But that would have meant taking himself out of the sales game. You don't pull Babe Ruth out of Game 7 of the World Series to fix the showers in the locker room. But you can send in his well-meaning, twenty-something son, right?

I was careful not to throw my weight around at first. Some of these guys were twice my age or older, and I wasn't about to tell them their business my first day on the job. As far as they knew, I wasn't even there to overhaul their entire operation. I was just there to do quality control on the product, soak up the wisdom of my elders, and learn the ropes a little.

This low-key strategy lasted about a week.

You have to realize that I'm just not the type of person who can keep his mouth shut. I don't just "go with the flow." My dad certainly knew this when he gave me the assignment. He didn't want a wallflower in charge of QC. He wanted a maniac.

When you're on the warehouse floor, you see everything that enters and exits. You see every bloodline on every fish, you feel if the shells of shrimp are cracked or solid, you smell how sweet and fresh the beautiful day boat scallops are, tasting them raw right out of the bucket to make sure you're getting the quality you expect—and the quality your customers expect.

I'm sure I rubbed a lot of my colleagues the wrong way. I *know for a fact* that I pissed off a lot of our suppliers, especially the ones that had gotten used to passing off bad product on us. I had to let them know that there was a new sheriff in town. That someone was going to hold our company and our products to a higher standard and would be scrutinizing every scrap of food that walked in our door.

And it was the same deal for anything that left our warehouse. Everything had to be perfect before it went out to a customer. No janky crab legs would ever make it into an order on my watch. That case of freezer-burnt sea bass would go into the trash before it went into a restaurant's kitchen. If I spotted a damp delivery box heading onto a truck, I'd go ballistic—replace it with a fresh one!

With the QC sorted out, I turned my attention to delivery logistics, which were in absolute shambles. I quickly determined that our truck drivers had way too much power. As main points of contact between us and the customers, they were obviously important, but that was no excuse to let them do whatever they wanted!

Under the system that was in place when I came in, they largely decided their own routes, horse-trading amongst themselves for whatever they thought would be more advantageous or convenient. So the product would be pulled from the warehouse and instead of going out immediately, it was left waiting on the loading docks for hours while the drivers haggled over who would be visiting which customers that day. ("Hey, you take my Upper East Side today, and I'll take both of your Jersey stops.") Sometimes they'd straight-up tell the dispatcher that there was a stop or two they wouldn't be making at all that day. ("I'll get to it tomorrow.") It was completely lawless, and it blew my mind that it was the system that had been in place for years. It was shocking that anything ever got delivered on time.

Letting drivers pick and choose like that is grossly inefficient. Winging it means unpredictable delivery times, which restaurants hate. If they're expecting a delivery in the morning, they might be planning to start prep on the product as soon as it gets there. They're going to be really pissed if their driver decides to call an audible and change his route, potentially shifting their delivery window to the afternoon, or even the next day.

We needed a better system. So I set out to devise one.

I took home all the paper invoices that were generated over six months. I'd spend my weekends poring over the documents, laying them out in a grid on the floor of my apartment. Then I went through and called every customer we delivered to, and asked them what their preferred delivery time was. With that info in hand, I started to organize each delivery stop by geography, requested time of day, and average size of order.

Working with our dispatcher, we fed everything into the computer. We split everything up into delivery zones. Manhattan was our busiest delivery area, so that got broken down even further into zones by individual neighborhoods. Then the other four outer boroughs were each their own zone. Westchester County and the suburbs north of NYC were another zone. Then out-of-state: Connecticut, New Jersey, Pennsylvania, Massachusetts—each became an individual zone.

It was organized and streamlined, and the best part was that once all the hard work of organizing it was done, the computer did all the day-to-day work! No more drivers haggling over routes. No more warehouse crew standing around drinking coffee and eating pastries while they waited for the drivers to finish their haggling. Instead, the sales people would place the orders and enter them into the computer, the computer would calculate the best routes, and the dispatcher would assign them. It was a perfect system.

And everyone hated it.

At first, anyway. Because here I was, a snot-nosed kid telling them they had to completely change the way they were doing things.

But I took their heat. Because I knew that my system worked, and they'd come around eventually. And guess what? It did, and they did.

Our customer service people in the office started high-fiving me every time I walked through, because they were thrilled that the phones had stopped ringing all day with customers asking "Where's my delivery?" The drivers grew to love it too, because even though they lost some of their autonomy, they realized that their days had gotten a lot better and less stressful. They were able to leave the warehouse on time, avoid getting caught in peak rush hour traffic, and finish their routes earlier.

Everyone eventually figured out that this new efficiency also led to more capacity on the truck for more deliveries. We were able to sell more, which meant more profits for the company, which led to more hours available for the drivers and warehouse workers, and therefore more money for them as well. Eventually we needed more trucks, and more drivers to run them, and more warehouse guys to fulfill them. We were growing the business simply by cleaning up our operations.

Looking back on it, sticking me in the warehouse was by far the best thing my father could have done for me. While there was no doubt that I'd eventually end up doing sales—my destination was predetermined by my last name—my particular route to that place was never going to be set in stone, and Val took special care to ensure that the road wouldn't be easy.

All said and done, it was three years before he'd even *entertain* the thought of me joining the sales team, and the truth is—I had to admit to myself—I was a lot better for it. Tackling the warehouse issues had helped me learn the business from the bottom up. That made me an infinitely better salesman down the line. Getting deep into the logistics meant that when a customer had a question, I had an instant answer for it. I could tell the customer with confidence when they could expect their deliveries, because I was the one that set the whole system up. Thanks to a later stint in the purchasing department, I could talk about what products we were expecting from where, during which season, and at what price.

The work had been painstaking, and time-consuming; if I'm being honest, it became a little bit of an obsession. A healthy obsession to be sure, but an obsession nonetheless. The nice thing was that despite some creakiness and inefficiencies, the company was healthy. The sales were good, the cashflow was strong, and all our problems were solvable. The solutions were surprisingly simple, too, so long as you did the work. Once you reconciled yourself to the fact that the effort just had to be expended and there was no shortcut around it, after that it was all just the meticulous application of math and logic and organization. Once your systems are set up just so, you can start to trust the process and things start taking care of themselves. Work gets easier and more fun. Everyone has a better time and makes more money. People who were wary of all your *big scary changes* started to come around.

Over those three years I looked over every aspect of our business. I knew that some people—not everyone, but some—had expected me to come in and coast and just wait it out until my father retired. I was determined from the moment I set foot on the warehouse floor to prove those people wrong. Even today, I don't consider myself The Boss.

Instead, I tell people, "I'm the best co-worker you'll ever have." I do the hard work. I never ask anyone to do anything that I wouldn't do myself. I encourage my employees to ask for help when they need it, and I'm happy to offer that help myself when I can.

Even though I have an office now, to this day there is no one place I spend more time in than the warehouse. It's still my baby, and I'm happy to say that it still continues to run better, smarter, and more efficiently all the time.

EVEN WITH MY undying love for the warehouse, I do admit that when I was finally brought up to the sales team it felt immensely gratifying, a little bit how I imagine a ballplayer getting called up from the minors to the big leagues might feel.

I was ready and eager to perform, to prove my worth yet again to a whole new set of doubters who just saw me as the pampered boss's kid.

As with my revamp of the warehouse, I had a system in mind. And again it was going to take a colossal amount of work to get off the ground. But hard work doesn't frighten me. Failure and rejection don't frighten me either. The only thing that frightens me is someone thinking, "He never even tried. He didn't want it enough."

Believe me, I wanted it.

I started my sales career with an old-fashioned, shoe leather strategy. Every Monday, Tuesday, and Wednesday I'd grab a yellow legal pad and head to downtown Manhattan, where I'd walk from east to west on every block, writing down every restaurant name, address, and phone number; making notes like what type of cuisine they served and how many customers they seated; reading menus posted in windows to see if they served any dishes that we might be able to supply ingredients for. Then on Thursday and Friday I'd head into the office and bury myself in the computer, further researching the names I'd gleaned, organizing my info and slowly building a database. I kept a tally of all my potential conquests, determining which ones were the most promising targets, and ranking them by how much money I estimated each could make me.

Once I had my list in place, it was cold-calling time.

This is one area of the business where determination pays off. These people are notoriously hard to reach. No one in the industry keeps what you might consider "standard" hours. These aren't nine-to-five guys. When you call the listed number, you're probably going to get a hostess, or the person taking orders for carryout and delivery. They're reluctant to connect you to anyone who's an actual decision-maker. In many cases they don't even know how to connect you to that person!

But I wouldn't take "no" for an answer. Yes, I know it's an old sales cliché, but there's a good reason everyone says it: it happens to be true. You really can't take "no" for an answer if you want to succeed. So I would call and call and call, and eventually fight my way to the purchaser, the chef, or the owner.

It can take weeks to even get on the phone with them, but once you're there you have a new set of problems to solve. These guys have notoriously high sales resistance. They're getting pitches constantly from all kinds of suppliers—not just seafood guys, but meat and produce and staffing agencies and cleaners and linen launderers and private trash collectors and tech bros who promise to revamp their online reservation-taking and guys who offer to haul away their used cooking oil, and so on and so on. Just pitch after pitch, all day long, so they have no qualms about saying "no" and hanging up on you. Which means you've got about eight seconds to grab their attention or you're going to lose them forever.

My strategy was always to try to dazzle them right off the bat with some impressive pricing. Even though we consider ourselves a premium, high-quality distributor with the best product out there, that's not something that gets your foot in the door with a new customer. No way. The only thing that gets their attention and keeps them on the phone is you telling them how you are going to save them money.

If I still had their attention at this point, this is where all the research I'd already put in would start to pay off. Before I called, I already knew the product that appeared most on their menu, and that's where I'd start to entice them.

Say, for example, that I know a restaurant has three or four shrimp dishes in their rotation. That's our starting point right there. I'd start by rattling off all our different sizes and styles of shrimp, and throwing out some tempting hints on pricing: *Which of these can you use? Why don't you let me come meet with you, and we'll take a look at your cooler and see what you've already got in there? I guarantee you I can do better on the price or the quality or both. So why don't I just drop by later this week? Whattaya say?*

Sometimes this initial come-on worked, but most of the time it didn't. If they gave me a firm "no," I'd back off—but just for a little while. A couple days or weeks later, I'd circle back. I found it was a good strategy to time my follow-ups to market fluctuations. Let's say that shrimp or lobster tails were suddenly spiking in price. That means the restaurant is suddenly paying their current supplier a lot more for the same amount of product, and there's no way they're happy about it. That's when I'd swoop in, hoping that their dissatisfaction would buy me another few minutes of precious time to get an audience: *Hey, I know you can't be happy paying that much. Well, we can give it to you cheaper, because we were smart enough to stock up when the price was still low and now we're sitting on a ton of supply. Why don't I send you a case or two, just to try, and we'll see how happy you are with your current guys after that?*

I was polite. I was friendly. But I was relentless. And thanks to my dad and my upbringing I had not only a knowledge of, but a genuine passion for the food. That made it easier to deal with these chefs. We'd connect on that level, food guy to food guy. We spoke the same language.

I got more comfortable in my role, but—crucially—I never let myself *feel* fully comfortable. I never allowed myself to coast. I closed deals like I had a chip on my shoulder, with the attitude that I always had something to prove. I didn't want to just skate by on my last name; I wanted to dominate the sales department so completely that there'd be no doubt that when it was my turn to take over the company, I deserved it. So I sold like a lunatic.

If I ever felt like I was in a rut with selling in the city, or I had a few irons that needed a little more time in the fire before I was ready to strike, I could always back off from the local scene and expand my attention further out, working to grow our footprint in territories that we didn't already have a huge presence in. The company had always sold to the tri-state area—New York, New Jersey, Connecticut—but I wanted more market share.

There are plenty of cities further afield that have the same cosmopolitan mix of restaurants as NYC, but they were never on our radar. The logistics of selling outside of our immediate geographic area just seemed too intimidating. But that didn't seem like a good enough reason to ignore a giant chunk of the country. Reaching out to markets like Vegas and Miami and Chicago made sense. Before I knew it, we were sending products all over the country.

I found selling outside of the east coast to be freeing, actually. The tri-state area is just riddled with competition that simply didn't exist in these new markets I was exploring. The sales came shockingly easy, as I reached out to chefs and owners who hadn't had much of a choice in distributors before, and were blown away by our pricing and selection. These people weren't dodging my calls or hanging up on me. They were actually excited to listen to my pitches!

As I CONTINUED boosting my stature at the company, there were a few bumps on the way. My ascent didn't sit well with everyone. I think there was initially a perception that I would phone it in, or even fall flat on my face. When it became clear that it wasn't going to quite go down like that, most people in the office came around, but there were one or two who kept grumbling. As I climbed the ranks even further, eventually becoming the top salesman after only a few years on the job, tensions boiled over.

The salesman that I'd surpassed to take the number-one spot quit in a fit of rage one day. I'd always suspected that he'd had designs of taking over the company himself one day, buying out my family entirely. My continuing success only proved that this wasn't going to be an option for him, and he couldn't take it.

I was actually a little sorry to see him go. He was a great salesman, and I would have happily kept him on, had he been willing to be a team player. But he let jealousy and pique get the better of him, and ultimately the company was stronger without him.

Ironically, after he left, I backed off the throttle a little. I felt like I had come along enough that I didn't have as much to prove anymore, personally, so I started worrying about what was best for the company as a whole. I set about helping my colleagues sell more, giving them advice, sharing some of my methods, attending pitch meetings with their potential customers, and helping them price out bid sheets.

Everyone—myself included—was able to put their egos in check and row in the same direction.

And guess what?

We all made a shitload more money!

Sales guys (and yes, until recently, it was an all-male sales force) that had been there for years, living comfortably but not particularly exceeding, suddenly found themselves rolling in it. With my sales philosophy and their willingness to take good advice instead of storming off like butthurt crybabies, we all won in the end.

It's been fifteen years now since I started in that warehouse, and I've taken my place at the top of the company. My father is semi-retired. He's still very much in the mix, of course—hustling is in his blood, and he can't stay out of the game entirely— but he's left the day-to-day with me. We're humming along nicely, but I'm always looking for ways to get bigger.

One shortcut I've found? Acquire the competition.

Three years prior to my joining the company, my dad had bought a distribution company that specialized in supplying Chinese and Asian restaurants. This had opened new markets to us, while helping us become even more efficient. While there's some overlap, the products requested by chefs cooking Eastern cuisine—especially the super-authentic Asian restaurants of the type you might find in an area like Flushing, Queens—tend to differ from the products requested by chefs cooking Western cuisines. For example, Asian restaurants want a lot of really small shrimp (like those little guys that go in Pad Thai), while most American recipes have no use for it. But a lot of our producers are looking to sell both big and small shrimp at the same time, to the same company. Now that we had the new distributor under our roof, we were able to accommodate those producers and take their whole load off their hands all at once, instead of picking and choosing certain sizes. That got us much better deals. As an added bonus, we'd also acquired the distributor's bilingual sales force, a necessity when dealing with chefs and owners who may not know English.

That's what a good acquisition can get you. You're not just buying up your competitors; you're using their skillset to shore up areas where you might be weak, or reach markets that you previously had no access to.

Once I took over, I followed my father's lead and got to work on some acquisitions of my own. A small distributor that I occasionally sold to was run by a pair of brothers: Dino and Nick. They were about my age and were also second-generation owners of a family business, having taken over for their father after he'd died unexpectedly.

I clicked immediately with the brothers, and knew that their company would be a perfect fit with mine. They dealt primarily with fresh, unfrozen product, while we were selling almost entirely high-end frozen products. The two businesses complemented each other perfectly.

I invited them to dinner one night, and just like that we cut a deal before the server even had time to bring the entrees out.

What I got out of this acquisition was priceless. Dino became not only my best employee, but practically family as well. Dino brought his customers over, of course, but even more valuable was his expertise in an entire area of business that we had only previously dipped our toes into. Overnight we were carrying fifty new items, and with our capital and buying power we could command better pricing and offer that to our customer base.

When I started with the company in 2006, we were doing about $25 million a year in revenue. By 2019, that had doubled to a little more than $50 million, our best year ever. With Dino at my side and my dad advising behind the scenes, I had no reason to doubt that the next would be even bigger than that.

Nothing could stop us from having our best year ever in 2020!

Right?

ONE OF MY favorite things about running a business is that I get to employ people. Every expansion we make, every extra account, every new product, every crate shipped—that means more employees. More drivers, more fish cutters, more truck loaders, more sales people, more hard-working men and women who depend on the company for their livelihoods. For food on their family's table.

I take this responsibility very seriously. I fully expect my employees to give their all, but it's a two-way street. As an employer, it's my job to have their backs, and to never leave them in the lurch.

Which brings us to COVID-19.

I probably caught wind of the disease a few weeks before it was on most people's radars. My Chinese salesmen who were still in touch with people from back home were getting a picture of how bad things were that the US media hadn't picked up on yet. My first thought was that it was definitely something to keep an eye on, since a lot of my supply chain runs through China and other Asian countries. But, like most of you, I never suspected it was anything that was going to severely impact my daily life, or cause any significant disruption to my business.

Flash forward to mid-March 2020. Almost overnight, my once-thriving little operation went from shipping 150,000 pounds of seafood a week to a meager 5,000.

The mighty torrent of my business slowed to a trickle.

This probably would have been a good time to panic. Most restaurants were closed, and showing no signs of reopening for dining in anytime soon. And a lot of the types of places I supplied weren't exactly takeout-friendly. Unless there was a proliferation of pizza places looking to add king crab legs or red snapper to their toppings list, it seemed that business was going to be slow—practically nonexistent—for the foreseeable future.

But panicking is not something I do.

Even before I was running it, I had grown up with this business. There were people working for me who I had literally known my entire life. These are good folks, hard workers who have been in the trenches with me for years. I wasn't about to abandon them just because we were taking the worst shelling in our history.

I resolved right then and there—no layoffs. No one would lose their jobs. No one would have their salary cut. No one would lose a shift.

My accountants were apoplectic, screaming at me about how dumb I was being.

"Do you know how much you're going to lose?"

"I don't want to know," I told them. "Don't bother telling me."

I knew I just had to take 2020 on the chin, like a big boy. Accept the fact that this was not going to be a banner year. I was confident that we could weather the storm. We were in good shape. We had the cash reserves we needed, because we'd been running lean and smart for years. Our books were tight.

So while some of my competitors cut and run, immediately closed their doors, did massive layoffs, and stiffed all their vendors—telling them they'd pay them thirty cents on the dollar or maybe even nothing at all—I took a different tack. First, I called an all-hands meeting at the warehouse. I gave a short speech, and told my employees that no one was going to lose their job: "I promise I'm going to protect you. All I ask is that you stick with me, have a little faith, and keep up a good attitude. We're going to get through this, together."

Next, my purchasers and I called all our vendors. I told them we'd pay every single invoice, no exceptions, and we'd continue to do so. They'd have nothing to worry about.

Then my salesmen and I called all our customers: *We know this is a tough time for you. We're here for you to help in whatever way we can. We're going to give you leeway on paying your bills. We're going to be responsive to your needs. If you want a different product than normal, one that's easier to sell for takeout, let's talk.*

With those affairs settled, I went about trying to replace at least a little bit of the revenue stream that we were losing out on. Our problem was that diners weren't buying anything from restaurants, so restaurants weren't buying from us. One obvious solution came to mind immediately: why not just go straight to the diners? Even if people weren't eating in restaurants, people still needed to eat, right?

So like so many others in the food industry, we would turn to home deliveries.

In a matter of days we pivoted our entire operation. We had to take stock of what we had, determine what might be most attractive to home cooks, and divvy it up into smaller portions—most people wouldn't be ordering an entire case like restaurants did.

Anyone who had been idled by the pandemic, I put to work in an impromptu marketing department. We went old-school, handing out fliers all over town: subway entrances, apartment building lobbies, hospitals, police precincts, fire houses. We revamped our website, offering customers the ability to order online with no minimum order size, and no delivery fees anywhere in the tri-state area.

Make no mistake—this was not a profitable endeavor, at this point. At best I expected to break even on this small-scale retailing. At worst I figured it was going to cost me more than it brought in. But I just wanted these guys working. Even if it meant spending my own money, it was worth it to me.

The amazing thing—the real silver lining of it all—is that it eventually caught on. We'd never done direct-to-consumer before, mostly because there was no reason. But after a few months of it, we got the hang of things. My brother-in-law Will was invaluable in figuring out the tech side, making a streamlined experience for customers. My sister-in-law Shelby, who is in charge of marketing, put in some incredible effort dealing with this influx of new customers. With their leadership and the hard work of my entire team, we came to the realization that direct-to-consumer could be a profitable operation all on its own. We'd been ignoring this market the whole time, but there was money for the taking. COVID had just been the kick in the butt we needed to force us to figure it out.

Even more than that, it was a huge morale boost. It's hard to overstate how scary that time was in New York City. Hospitals were full, people were dying, everything felt like it was up in the air and there was no sense of when things would get better. But getting our retail up and running gave all of us a purpose and something to focus on besides the constant flow of bad news. Our shared attempt to keep the business together had brought all of us closer, and the culture at our company was stronger than ever.

Now, as I write this in fall of 2021, there's a feeling of normalcy starting to creep back in. Restaurants are open, and we're busier than ever. The future is looking really bright.

I lost a lot of money in 2020, but what I found out about myself and my employees along the way may end up making it all worthwhile in the long run.

I'VE DEVELOPED SORT of a personal business philosophy over the years. There are three tenets:

1. Always do the right thing.
2. Work well with others.
3. Make as much money as humanly possible.

In my experience, concentrating on no. 1 and no. 2 are the most important parts. If you do those properly, no. 3 will take care of itself. When you work hard, and you treat people with respect—your customers, your suppliers, *and* your employees—money is simply the byproduct of that.

Some people put no. 3 first, and completely ignore no. 1 and no. 2. While that may work for them in the short run, these out-of-whack priorities will eventually catch up with them and lead to disaster.

I've also found that it's important to enjoy your work, and do what you can to make sure those around you enjoy their work as well. Attitude goes a long way, and developing a fun atmosphere has side benefits that might not always be visible on a spreadsheet. A company with a good culture has better morale, and that will always lead to higher profits than a company where everyone is miserable.

I was raised to care about food—the consumption of it, naturally, but also the preparation; the history; and the routines and traditions that surround it. The way that every culture puts their own spin on it, and it becomes something that defines them.

I'm proud to be a part of this industry that I love. And that was one of my main motivations for writing this book: I want you, the reader, to understand it, learn about it, and come to love it in the same way that I do.

Chapter 4

FRESH OUT OF LUCK: WHY YOUR MENU IS A DIRTY LIAR

WITHOUT A DOUBT, the biggest success story of the past two decades in my industry has been the Chilean sea bass.

It ain't much to look at, I'll tell you that much. It's a butt-ugly fish, five feet long and plump, covered in corpse-gray scales, with a gaping mouth and fat lips and weird, dead eyes with giant pupils that are usually a startling shade of blue. It has a row of creepy, tiny little sharp teeth, which is probably what caused fishermen to name it the "toothfish." Patagonian toothfish, to be exact, after the waters off of the southern peninsula of South America where it was first caught.

Patagonian toothfish, of course, didn't sound remotely appetizing to anyone, which is how a guy named Lee Lantz found himself stuck with forty thousand unsold pounds of the stuff in the late seventies. He had imported it to Los Angeles, thinking that the mild, flaky white flesh would be a perfect fit for American palates, but he was having trouble unloading it under its true name. It needed a rebrand.

A toothfish is technically a type of cod, but Lantz figured that sea bass sounded more appealing. And since most Americans couldn't come close to picking out the Patagonian peninsula on a map, Lantz decided that he needed to peg the fish to a more well-known locale. Chile wasn't quite where the fish came from, but it was close enough. It was a place that sounded suitably exotic, and if most Americans still probably couldn't even pick that country out on a map, at the very least they could probably name the correct hemisphere.

So the Chilean Sea Bass was born. Some brilliant marketing turned a poorly-regarded bottom-feeder—that even the working-class locals would throw back if they accidentally caught it—into the hottest, trendiest, most sought-after fish in the world.

It certainly helps that it's a delicious piece of seafood. Unlike a lot of other white fish, the Chilean Sea Bass is ultra-fatty. It might make your personal trainer cringe, but it will make your chef (and your mouth) quite happy. The high fat content acts as sort of an insurance policy for the fish, making it virtually impossible to overcook. Unlike many other kinds of fish, you can blast Chilean filets with any type of heat you can think of, and unless it is literally on fire when you're done with it, chances are you are going to have a moist, delicious dinner. All that fat renders into scrumptious, buttery goodness that lurks between the mild, non-fishy, firm white flakes.

Is your mouth watering yet? It should be. Wouldn't you like some freshly caught, straight off the boat, never-frozen Chilean sea bass right now? I know I would!

But you can't have any.

Neither can I.

Neither can *anyone* in the United States. Because for Chilean sea bass, along with almost every other single type of fish that enters this country from foreign waters, the FDA requires that the fish be frozen before being served for human consumption.

There is, effectively, no such thing as fresh Chilean sea bass.

Wait, what's that?

Your menu says it's "fresh"?

I'm here to tell you that your menu is a dirty fucking liar.

BEFORE WE DELVE more into this ugly truth—this dirty little not-so-secret reality of the industry—we need to talk about what "frozen" means.

We're not talking about you pouring your leftover, Super-Bowl-party batch of chili into a flimsy piece of IKEA tupperware and sticking it into the dinky combo fridge/freezer in your kitchen, only to dig it out six months later, reheating and choking down the freezer-burned slop on a night you're too lazy to call for a pizza.

No, it's not that kind of frozen.

We're talking about giant blast freezers, commercial behemoths that blow continuous streams of cold air over the fish, freezing it nearly instantaneously to temperatures as nut-shrivelingly low as 70 degrees below zero. At that temperature, stored and treated properly, fish can last for—I shit you not—up to two years before being served, with no noticeable loss of quality after the defrost.

I know it sounds unbelievable. We as a country are so conditioned to equate "fresh" with "quality" that it's second-nature to automatically reject frozen.

Unbeknownst to most of us, we've been eating mostly frozen all along. Our entire lives. Without realizing it.

Aside from lobster and shellfish (which are often alive mere minutes before being served to you) and unless you live in one of a handful of coastal towns with strong fishing industries, there's a pretty good chance that you've actually never had a "fresh" fish.

And this is true industry-wide—from the lowliest Red Lobster or Long John Silver's, all the way up to the highest of the high-end sushi joints.

I have a good friend and loyal customer, a top Manhattan celebrity chef, who knows a thing or two about good fish. And he *swears* he can't tell the difference, even in a blind taste test, between fresh and frozen—as long as the fish is frozen properly and treated well at all steps of the process.

It's when the fish is not treated properly that we run into problems.

Fish should be thawed gently, and gradually, in a climate-controlled environment. It should take a day or two. But time is of the essence in the restaurant industry, so a lot of the time they'll just dunk frozen fillets in some hot water, or even microwave them. Compounding the issue, it's also a widespread practice at restaurants to re-freeze unsold product.

This happens, mind you, after the product was initially received frozen from the distributor, and then defrosted by the restaurant. If it fails to move after a few days on the menu, often the kitchen will simply place it back in the cooler and worry about it later.

The problem is, you can't just put that genie back in the bottle. When it comes to frozen seafood, there's such a thing as diminishing returns. The first time a fish defrosts (properly defrosts, not microwaved), it's basically at 100 percent. No noticeable loss of quality. That's not so the second time around. Even with optimal conditions, the refreeze is always going to be more stressful on the fish than the first freeze was. That means after the second defrost, it's not going to bounce back as strongly. The texture suffers, the taste suffers—it's noticeably worse.

And that would be under perfect re-freezing conditions, which in a restaurant setting is pretty much a fantasy. Most restaurants don't have a dedicated blast freezer, capable of flash-freezing fish. What they've got is the same walk-ins that they use to freeze everything else. You know— the one that's right next to the hot kitchen, barely able to maintain below-freezing temps because every time the busboy walks in to grab a bag of ice he lets all the cold air out.

Product that's re-frozen under those conditions is basically being murdered.

That's right. You're all accessories to fish murder.

It mostly comes down to freezing speed. Without getting too technical about it: Fast is good. Slow is bad. When you freeze something, all the water inside is converted to ice. This ice is in the form of crystals. Crystals are sharp.

When you freeze a piece of fish quickly, it ends up with small ice crystals that don't do a lot of damage. You freeze it slow? It forms giant ice crystals. Thousands of frigid daggers just stabbing the bejeezus out of this beautiful piece of protein, turning it to absolute mushy bullshit.

That said, it's still usually safe to eat at this point. You really don't want it as an entree anymore, though some restaurants with lax standards will still serve it as such. The more ethical establishments won't serve it as an entree, but they will get creative and find a use for it. It becomes the seafood equivalent of "mystery meat"—perhaps shredded and bulking up the spicy tuna roll mixture, or cubed and floating in a chowder.

So BACK TO your lying menu—why does it say "fresh" next to certain items that by definition cannot be fresh? Why do chefs and owners continue to advertise things that they blatantly know to be false? Well, a few reasons.

The first is because they believe no one will ever call them on it. And they're right! As we've already covered, if the chef has done his job right, no one will be able to tell the difference from the taste and texture alone. Even if a diner had the requisite knowledge to ask the right questions, they're usually too polite or non-confrontational to press their server on the point. And frankly, most servers would probably be unaware that the dish was anything less than advertised.

So the restaurateur can safely assume that they'll get away with it.

Look at it from their point of view: if calling the Chilean sea bass "fresh" on the menu sells a few more plates, it's worth it. *What's the harm in a little white lie,* they might think, *if it makes the dish sound more appetizing?*

I've also heard this dubious argument from a restaurant owner: "fresh" can mean a lot of things. They're technically correct: at its most basic, the word "fresh" simply means "not spoiled." As long as a restaurant is serving fish that is not *actively rotting,* they can delude themselves into thinking they're not being dishonest.

Of course, that's not our common understanding of "fresh." In America, when we see "fresh fish" on a menu, we expect fish that was caught recently, and has never been frozen. I believe that we as an industry should strive to educate the public about what they're getting. Fresh fish is great. Frozen can be great too, under the right circumstances. Either way, we owe it to the customers to give them full disclosure every step of the way.

I know I'm being pretty harsh on chefs and owners here, so I should concede that sometimes the fault lies with my side of things. Sometimes the restaurants won't even be aware that their product had been previously frozen. They've been taken in by one of my less scrupulous peers, someone who buys fish frozen, defrosts it themselves, then sells it to restaurants as "fresh," at a premium price. This is more common than people in my industry like to admit, and frankly it's depressing.

Personally, I'd rather close my doors tomorrow and start turning tricks with lonely sailors down by the docks for a living than do something dishonest like that, but again that's an uncomfortable reality of the industry.

So here's your strategy going forward: ignore the word "fresh" on the menu. It's essentially meaningless. Unless the fish is caught locally, there is a very slim chance that it's actually fresh, never-frozen. (And even if the menu says "local," there's still a pretty decent chance that's a lie.)

Instead, ask your waiter when the fish came in. Ideally, you want to hear, "It just came in today." If the answer is "yesterday," that's also not terrible. If the answer is "a few days ago" or even "I don't know," well, then you're probably better off ordering the chicken.

ASIDE FROM HAVING your head on a swivel looking for the word "fresh," which we've established is often a lie, there are certain other things you should look for when reading a restaurant menu. Little things, to be sure, but if you can crack the code you can save money and ensure that you get the best possible meal.

1. LOCATION COUNTS

If you're dining in a restaurant in the northeast, do you really want those Littlenecks from Florida? Or that shrimp from the Gulf? Or those California oysters? Probably not. At least not unless you're very, very confident in the fact that the restaurant you're dining in takes care with its product. And even then, maybe think twice. The supply chain can be long and circuitous. The longer seafood has to travel, the more hands it passes through, and the greater chance some of those hands were doing something wrong.

The other side of the coin is that if there's no source location at all associated with the dish, that could also be a warning sign. At the very least the server or chef should be able to tell you where exactly the product came from. If they don't know, or they won't tell you, then it's an indication that they're not keeping close tabs on their inventory, and that's a huge red flag.

2. BEWARE OF SAUCES
Heavy cream sauces, chunky fruit salsas, spicy mayo, layers of avocado with crunchy bits sprinkled on top—these are all distractions, meant to cover up the quality of the product underneath. It's not a guarantee that the tuna in your sushi roll is bad, but it's certainly much easier for chefs to hide a multitude of sins underneath a thick layer of other strong flavors, potentially allowing them to charge what they want while masking a subpar product. Tread carefully.

3. DITTO CRUSTING
Potato-crusted, panko-crusted, pistachio-crusted, battered and deep-fried? Same deal. Someone in the industry whose opinion I trust wholeheartedly once told me that this coating was a trick to not only make the fish look bigger on the plate, but also gave the perception of added value, allowing them to charge more. Tacking on these ingredients costs next to nothing and is able to disguise, if necessary, bad product, so I generally avoid dishes that incorporate them. Not that these dishes can't be delicious sometimes—who doesn't like fried crispy things? But just as often the crusting is counterproductive, as the delicate taste of the fish is overpowered by the coating, and the crispiness destroys the texture and integrity.

4. . . . AND ALSO STUFFING
If you encounter any formulation where X is stuffed into Y, it's probably best to back away slowly and quietly. Again, it sounds delicious, but it's just an excuse to charge you more for less. Because you can be certain they're not saving their best quality ingredients for the crab-stuffed sole, or lobster-stuffed shrimp, or shrimp-stuffed mahi, or whatever combination they're pushing. The stuffing is not going to be particularly good quality, and neither is the *stuffee* for that matter.

5. NEVER GET THE RISOTTO SPECIAL

One thing that nearly every chef I've ever spoken to agrees on—if they have leftover product they're trying to get rid of, maybe a day or two past prime, and they don't feel like freezing it, they simply toss it in a risotto along with a tiny bit of lobster meat and lots of mushrooms.

Sorry to burst your bubble, but the lobster, scallop, and mushroom risotto that you were so excited about has barely any lobster, week-old scallops, and enough mushrooms and butter and white wine to drown out any funky flavors.

Truthfully, that's not going to kill you. It kind of sounds delicious, actually. I'd probably eat the shit out of that right now. But you should go into this thing eyes wide open. I want you to know exactly what you're getting into when you order that risotto special.

6. DON'T EVEN GET ME STARTED ON "MARKET PRICE"

Sorry to go off on this one, but it's my book so you'll have to indulge me: Market Price is the number-one menu scam. It's maybe even the biggest ripoff in the entire restaurant industry. When you see "MP" on a menu, it's a sure sign that your wallet is about to be absolutely violated. Market Price is simply the restaurant industry preying on the general public's ignorance of seafood.

The fact of the matter is that, thanks to the aforementioned advances in freezing technology, the supply of most types of fish is relatively stable year round. Even if a restaurant manages to get some fresh stuff into their rotation, the price should not differ wildly from the price of the flash-frozen product. So the problem is that market prices are theoretically in place to counteract a fluctuating market—but only in the rarest circumstances today do markets actually fluctuate. So you're not actually paying "market price." You're paying whatever the restaurant thinks you should pay. And you can bet it's a lot, too. Because if it wasn't, they'd list it with the regularly-priced dishes.

Market price is simply a way of hiding sticker shock. Period. End of story. Allen has spoken.

If you knew that swordfish entrée was going to cost you $38, you'd probably gravitate to something else. And sure, you could always ask the waiter, but who wants to risk looking like a cheapskate in front of your friends, business associates, or date? Restaurants are banking on the fact that you're going to feel awkward about asking the price, so by the time you realize how much you shelled out for your dinner, the server is already waiting to swipe your credit card, and there's nothing you can do but hand it over and bite your tongue. This goes for most types of dishes you'd find under the market price heading, which is why I'd avoid that section of the menu at all costs.

There is an exception, a category that actually *is* affected by the ups and downs of the seasons, and the prices that fishermen are charging on the docks—and that's live seafood. We're talking lobster, oyster, crab, clams, anything that would come on a raw bar platter. But even those, thanks to savvy fishery management and advanced harvesting techniques, have enjoyed relatively stable—and low—prices in recent years.

For example, in 2012, an especially abundant harvest in Maine dropped lobster prices to $1.35 a pound, wholesale. The lobstermen were practically giving it away to tourists and passersby who were hanging out on the docks, just to get it off their hands.

But hey, a dip in the wholesale price has gotta be great news for diners, right? If "market price" actually means that the price at a restaurant goes up and down accordingly, then we should be seeing the price of a lobster dinner drop down to about the level of a Big Mac SuperSize combo, right?

Do you think that's what happened in 2012?

Of course not.

What actually happened, is that most restaurants declined to lower their "market prices" to account for the cheaper product. As *Slate Magazine* noted at the time:

> When lobster prices rise, the market price does rise with them. . . . But the ratchet really only goes in one direction. When upward price swings squeeze margins enough, restaurants raise prices. But falling retail lobster prices generate big restaurant profits, angry lobstermen, and vaguely disappointed tourists.

I'm a fan of lobster as much as the next guy. Which is to say I find it more than a little overrated, but will gladly scarf one down if it's put in front of me. But I'll never order one at a market price establishment without first reconciling myself to the fact that I'm going to pay out the nose; and it's going to be a number that has very little—if any—relation to what the actual product cost the restaurant. Once I get that in my head, I can at least attempt to enjoy my meal.

Pass the melted butter, please.

BEWARE OF ADD-ONS

One last scam to be on the lookout for: a lot of high-end restaurants will try to upsell you with fancy toppings added on to already-expensive dishes. You see this a lot with ingredients like foie gras, caviar, and especially truffles. The genius of this scam is that a lot of the time these add-ons aren't even listed on the menu. The servers are instructed to present them while they're taking your order, pitching the ingredient as something special that just happened to show up in the kitchen that morning. "Oh, we have some really great white truffles that just came in today. Would you like some shaved over your risotto?"

That's hard to say no to, because truffles are obviously delicious. And again, it's equally hard to ask the price. When you're on the spot and the whole table is listening to your order, asking the price might seem gauche. Or worse, if you ask the price and then decline the add-on, you really look like a miser. (Even though it's a perfectly sane decision to not want to pay $50 for a few limp fungus shavings, no matter how tasty they might be.)

Even more alarming is the roving truffle shaver. This is when your entrees are already at your table, and a server or maitre'd shows up with the truffle and the little wooden shaver already in hand. That's even harder to turn down, especially since by that point in the meal your table is probably already a bottle-of-wine-or-two deep. When your check comes and it's $300 more than you expected because everyone at the table said yes to the truffle man, there's nothing left to do but grumble about it and take the hit to your wallet.

There are several restaurants that are notorious for this practice, but one of my favorite stories, as widely covered by bloggers at the time, comes from a downtown Manhattan spot called The Waverly Inn. Owned by a famous magazine editor, it became an instant celeb-filled hotspot when it opened in the mid-aughts. One of their most popular dishes was a gourmet take on macaroni-and-cheese that clocked in at $55. Even though the standard order was already flavored with truffle oil, they'd still try to upsell you with the fresh truffle shaving. If you decided to partake, when the check showed up at the end of the meal you'd realize much to your chagrin that you just spent $95 on a side dish that you can get in a little blue box in the grocery store for 99 cents.

That's why whenever I see the truffle guy come my way I wave him off. The only add-on I like these days is the Parmesan cheese at an old-school red sauce Italian joint. That doesn't cost a thing.

So we've gone through a lot of what *not* to do, so far. I hope I haven't turned you off of seafood or restaurants entirely. There's a lot of good stuff to be had out there.

In general, you're better off keeping it simple. Simple preparations, limited ingredients, minimum sauces or toppings. Most of the time, if the product is really good, all it needs is a quick sear on the grill along with some salt, pepper, and maybe a squeeze of lemon or a pat of butter. And that's it. Let the integrity of the fish stand on its own.

The server or the chef should be able to tell you exactly where the fish is from, and not blow smoke up your ass about whether or not it was frozen. If you let them know that you're fully aware that frozen can be of the highest quality, then they'll know they're dealing with a knowledgeable customer. And if they have nothing to hide, and are proud of their product—fresh or frozen—they should have no problem filling you in on all the gory details.

Your menu is a giant liar, it's true—but that's not necessarily something to get mad about. Because a menu is also a marketing document. It's going to put the best possible spin on products it's selling. You wouldn't take a television commercial at face value, right? You shouldn't take a menu for its word either. A menu should be a jumping off point, a way to kickstart a conversation with the restaurant about what's really going on with your food.

It might take some work on your part. You have to be sort of a food detective, and you have to read between the lines a little bit. But be honest with me—don't you think you're worth it?

CHAPTER 5

ACT LIKE YOU'VE BEEN HERE BEFORE, DAMMIT: BECOMING A "REGULAR" WITH A REGULAR-GUY'S WALLET

EVERYONE NEEDS A place where they're considered a "regular."

You know what I'm talking about—a restaurant or bar where you know you can always walk in and no matter the time of day, or how busy the place is, the staff will drop everything to accommodate you and your guests.

Getting to be a regular is pretty easy:

Step one: find a place.
Step two: go there a lot.
Step three: drop thousands of dollars.

Oh yeah, step three is the catch.

But what if I told you that step three wasn't necessary? It's always an option, to be sure. And it's a fine shortcut if you're impatient and blessed with a large wallet.

But it's not the only way to fly.

Before we get into all of that though, let's tackle the first two steps.

Step one is target selection. My best advice here is find something close to where you live. There's a couple obvious reasons for this. The convenience factor, of course. You want a place that's easy to get to so you're more inclined to do so as often as possible. If you're anything like me, you're going to be spending some late (possibly drunken) nights at this place, so it pays to be a short walk/Uber ride away from your comfy bed.

Being close also makes it easier to go spur of the moment, which should be one of the perks of this venue in the first place—you can always just drop in, and even if the place normally requires reservations, no reservations are necessary.

A location close to where you work is also an option, but it's never as desirable because then you're more limited to it being just a worknight hang. Not a bad thing to have, to be sure, but definitely less versatile than a seven-day-a-week option. (Plus, you want this to be a place you can go to relax and be yourself. If you're constantly at risk of being surprised by your coworkers or your boss, that might not fly.)

As far as type of venue, you want something that matches your vibe. If you're a dive bar aficionado, that's great. If you're more into upscale restaurants, that's fine too. I'd just steer clear of choosing one of the ultra-fancy, white tablecloth, 10-course prix-fixe-type restaurants. Those are great on their own terms, but those are also the types of places that your *regular* status can only get you so far. They're booked up weeks, sometimes months in advance, and even if you're best friends with the maitre'd they're still not going to bump the table full of rich Wall Street assholes who are about to drop five-figures on wine pairings.

My strategy is to find a mid-range restaurant. Not too expensive, but not cheap either. Like the restaurant you'd maybe take someone on a first date. A fun, lively atmosphere, but not music blasting so loud you can't hear yourself think and a floor sticky with beer and blood from recent fights.

Step two: go a lot.

That's pretty self-explanatory, right? If you're going to be a *regular*, you have to go *regularly*.

How often, you ask? I'd say every other week, minimum. At least at the beginning, anyway. Once you've achieved your status (which you'll do faster than you think, maybe after just three or four visits) you can dial that down to less, once a month or so. Just check in periodically enough that they don't forget you.

Can you go too often? I struggled with this question a bit, mostly because I've been known to frequent some of my haunts three or four times a week. But I'd say that when you're still getting to know a place and its staff, show a bit of restraint. Twice a week is probably as much as I'd push it at the beginning, lest they start to think you're a weirdo. (Later on, when they actually *know for sure* that you're a weirdo, but still like you anyway, that's when you can feel comfortable, for example, showing up five nights in a row.)

(You don't have to commit to a full meal every time you stop in, either, especially if you find yourself going a lot. Just a quick drink or two, or an appetizer should suffice. There was a bar in Tribeca where I used to live that I'd just pop in to say "hi" on my way to the subway sometimes, shoot the shit for ten minutes or so, then go on my way.)

Okay, now onto step three. Like I said before, if every time you walk into the restaurant you flash a bunch of cash around, ostentatiously tip every hostess, bartender, and server, and order every item on the menu plus a pricey bottle of wine—yeah, they're going to remember you, and quickly—probably after just one or two visits. And sure, they're going to kiss your ass every time you come after that. But I'm telling you right now it's not going to be real affection. They're not going to actually like you for you. They're just going to like your money. I'm sure that's fine with some sociopaths out there. And God knows that NYC, in particular, certainly has its share of cold-blooded weirdos with plenty of money.

But for the rest of us, the goal shouldn't be to buy affection. It's something that should be earned. Like most good things in life, it will be way more meaningful and longer-lasting if you work hard to get it.

Essentially, I'm telling you to use your charm, not your charge card.

As someone who is blessed with both money AND a winning, rakish personality, I always prefer to use the latter to win people over. It's more fun, it's more rewarding, and it has the wonderful side effect of making you some lifelong friends along the way.

So here's what to do.

The most important thing is to be friendly and confident to the staff. Always, always, always. Being a dick to them will get you nowhere. They won't think it's funny, they won't think you're cool, they won't think it's cute. They'll just think you're a dick.

Restaurant people are some of the hardest-working, most underpaid, most mistreated people in the entire workforce, and if you add to their burden by being a pain in their ass, you're a terrible person.

Now, that said, if you want to be dickish to the *other customers*, that might actually win you some points.

Not to their faces, mind you. You're not trying to pick a fight here. But the fastest way to give yourself an *in* with a bar or restaurant staff—to let them know you're on *their* side—is to unite with them against their common enemy: their patrons.

Let me give you an example. When I'm talking to my server, I always make a point of poking fun at the other tables. Gentle stuff, at first, please. (When you know the server a little better and have a read on their sense of humor and whether or not they take offense easily, you can get *really mean*, if you want.) To start, you can make a dumb comment like "Ooh, what's that table ordering over there? I want to judge them."

Same thing with bartenders. They love it when you commiserate with them about the drunk idiots they've been serving all night. "Hey, Mr. White Claw at the end of the bar there thinks he's going home with that girl he's been chatting up, but I guarantee you he's definitely not." These little comments and inside jokes are a great way to break the ice and get the staff to warm up to you immediately.

Another way—defer to their expertise. When I'm at a new place and someone takes my order, the first thing I always say in reply is "What do you like?" Even if I know exactly what I'm going to order, I still ask. When you ask for people's advice, they are more than willing to give it to you. And I find that they're honest more often than not, and will happily steer you to the good stuff on the menu, and not—as you might expect—to just the most expensive items.

It's a good strategy because it helps you build a rapport, and it's flattering to them. It makes them feel like a dining expert (which they actually are) and not just like a robot who brings plates (which is how many people treat them).

The added benefit of this is that it really is useful for finding otherwise-overlooked hidden gems on menus. Same thing with the barkeep too—they might have a favorite cocktail, or know of a really good, under-the-radar bottle of something or other, or have some other advanced knowledge that you do not possess. So I like to let them run free.

Being a regular is all about building relationships. And we all know that relationships are built on trust. Well, there's no better way to convey that you trust someone than telling them, "I need you to help me decide what is going to go into my stomach tonight."

If a server tries to steer you toward the special, let them. The specials are "special" for a reason, and that's usually because they are designed to make money for the restaurant. Like they've got a surplus case of something they need to use up, or their supplier gave them a really good deal on an ingredient or something like that. Ordering the special is another way of showing that you are there to be a friend to the restaurant.

Obviously, another thing that screams "friend" is money. So let's talk tipping. You should tip generously.

Period.

None of this bullshit "well, the service was okay, but not great, so I'm tipping 12.5%". No. Stop. Don't do that. If you ever find yourself pulling out the calculator on your phone to figure out the tip, you're doing it wrong.

Twenty percent is the minimum. Let me say that again: 20 percent *minimum*. That's no matter the venue, no matter where you are in the country. Whether you're at a Waffle House off the interstate in Indiana or the French Laundry in Napa Valley or anywhere in between, it's a 20 percent tip. If you can't afford that, then you can't afford to go out. Period.

Twenty percent has the added benefit of being ridiculously easy to figure out, even for math-phobes like myself. If the bill is $120, ten percent of that is $12. Double that to get $24. (And even then you should probably tip $30 anyway for good measure, but I digress . . .)

So yes, my rule is to tip generously—but not too generously. You don't want to give the wrong impression that you're trying to buy their love. You don't want to set a precedent, giving the expectation that you're going to be heavy-handed with the cash every single meal. But you do want to let them know that you appreciate their work, and that you'll always treat them fairly.

If all else fails, there's one last surefire method I know of to get the servers on your side: show them pictures of your dogs. I don't know why this works, but it always does. If you don't have dogs, I recommend you get some. If that's not an option, well, don't tell anyone I gave you permission to do this, but Google Image Search is always a couple clicks away.

I LIVED IN TRIBECA in lower Manhattan for years, in a high-rise on Duane Street. It was definitely a great neighborhood with incredible restaurants, but I still bent my own rule and became a regular at a place that was a few neighborhoods further uptown.

Toro, on 10th Avenue in the Meatpacking District, was this insanely good tapas place, run by a group out of Boston. The food and atmosphere was so excellent that it wasn't uncommon for me to go three times a week. But what really kept me coming back was the people. It was a large space, covered by a ton of staffers, but I made it my mission to get to know everyone. And once they got to know me in return, it was like unlocking the key to a secret club. The hostesses were so kind, and the barkeeps knew exactly what I liked to drink and always had my scotch on the rocks ready for me moments after I walked in. I knew every server and every bus boy by name, and they knew me. It was like *Cheers* but with way more *jamón ibérico*.

When you get to know everyone who works there, not only do you not have to wait for a table, but you get the pick of the litter. They're not going to jam you back by the restrooms, or the busboy station. Toro, like many restaurants of its caliber, would hold tables for their regular clientele or special guests, and after a while I even developed a favorite table within the restaurant that was almost always made available for me.

Another place I frequented in those days was Rebelle, a cozy French restaurant on the Bowery that was a wine-lover's paradise. They had a bread course that was insane, a beautiful sourdough toast with a foie gras torchon. When I first met my wife and was still trying to impress her, I'd take her to Rebelle, where we'd start and end every meal with the toast and torchon. It was that good. Naturally, I got to know the staff there as well, which became very useful as I continued to woo my future bride. We were on a date one time, nearing the end of our meal, when the chef came to our table and told us he had something special he was working on. It wasn't on the menu yet, he explained, but he wanted us to try it and give our honest feedback.

A few minutes later he sent out an incredible dessert: a foie gras mousse, infused with fresh strawberries. I'd never tasted anything like it. It was decadent and delicious, but not overly rich, with the mellow notes of the berries and their acidity and sweetness perfectly cutting through the foie. Caylin and I practically licked our plates clean.

I guess that was the positive feedback the chef was looking for, because the dish showed up on the permanent menu a few weeks later.

When you're truly a regular at a restaurant, you don't just get to know the servers and front-of-house people. You get to know the people in the kitchen as well, the chefs and the sous-chefs and all the cooks. You don't see them as much, but they know when you're there because the servers tell them. I find that attempting to impress the regulars is something that causes a lot of kitchens to up their game. Most chefs have a bit of swagger to them, and can't help but show off a little, especially in front of customers they know will appreciate it.

Another time at Toro, the chef Jamie Bissonnette came to the table where my wife and I were sitting bearing a very peculiar gift—a roasted pig's tail. That wasn't something he was even considering putting on the menu. He just knew that I'd like it, even though most Americans are pretty squeamish about offal or cuts of meat that are a little off the beaten path. "This is the only one of these in the kitchen tonight," he explained, and he didn't want it to go to waste. Caylin and I picked that tail clean of every delicious morsel.

Maybe the best thing I'd get to sample off-menu on occasion would be a plate or two from the "family meal." That's the food that the staff cooks for itself in the late afternoon before dinner service starts. Usually it's something that's relatively simple to make, because nobody wants to work up too much of a sweat before being crushed with orders from paying customers for several hours. But, as you might expect from a group of world-class cooks, they're always trying to one-up each other, so what's supposed to be an easy, filling meal can end up being a dazzling display of cooking acumen. We're talking the most amped-up, gourmet versions of staple dishes like spaghetti and meatballs or grilled cheese.

My former Manhattan go-to restaurants are both closed now. Rebelle shuttered in 2017, a victim of the brutal realities of Manhattan real estate. Toro thrived a whole lot longer, but couldn't survive the pandemic, closing its doors for good a few weeks after indoor dining was shut down in March 2020. I mourn both of them, but I don't consider all the time I spent getting to know the people there as a wasted effort. The restaurant industry is small, even in a place as big as New York, and it's exciting to know that any time I walk into a new place for the first time there's a decent chance I'll see one of my friends and be instantly elevated to regular status again.

I don't live in Manhattan anymore, but I still have a local favorite in my old Tribeca stomping grounds: Wolfgang's Steakhouse. This is a mini-chain, started by the guy who used to be the head waiter at the Brooklyn landmark Peter Luger Steakhouse. Luger's is famous for its porterhouses, which are dry-aged and seared under a scorching hot broiler, seasoned simply with salt and melted butter, then pre-sliced before being brought to your table, still sizzling. Luger's is also legendary for having a decidedly un-charming atmosphere, service that can best be described as "gruff and businesslike," along with the consumer-unfriendly policy of not accepting credit cards. For years they were only cash, check, or their own house-issued card that you could only use there.

Wolfgang's takes the same approach to meat as the place that spawned it, but smooths off the rough edges of Luger's hospitality for a more refined dining experience. I like to bring co-workers there, or my wife, or even just treat myself to a meal at the bar. No matter how big or small my party, Ed the manager will always greet me almost immediately and usher me to the seat of my choice where a scotch on the rocks will be waiting.

I end every meal at Wolfgang's with their crazy-good apple strudel, served with a beautiful mound of fluffy whipped cream on the side— they call it "schlag." And in what might be my favorite "regular" perk in my entire dining life, they always give me plenty of extra schlag.

WOLFGANG'S IS OBVIOUSLY a higher-end venue, but the same rules to being a regular apply anywhere, down to the lowliest dive bar. Despite my deep love for the restaurant industry, I've always been a bar guy. And New York is a great bar town, maybe the greatest in the world. The combination of thousands of options, a generously-late closing time (4:00 a.m.!), and the fact that nobody has to drive home afterward makes this city a paradise for bar lovers.

My personal favorite type of bar is a classic Irish pub. Dark inside, lots of polished wood on every surface, knick-knacks and memorabilia adorning the bar-back, and lots of colorful personalities in attendance. For an added bonus, I like to frequent bars that are known as hang-outs for restaurant industry types. All the servers and cooks tend to get off around eleven or midnight, and they need places to come down from the adrenaline high of dinner service. If you can get in with a crowd of restaurant people after-hours, that's like unlocking an entirely new level of regulardom. When off-duty industry folks visit other restaurants or bars, they get perks and treatment that rival that of the biggest celebs in the world.

And I'll tell you, those people go *hard*. They'll often blow right through the 4:00 a.m. last call. The bartender will kick out all the civilians but let his fellow service employees stay as late as they want, and the party sometimes continues into the morning light as everyone decamps for a twenty-four-hour diner to soak up the night's booze with a life-saving helping of pancakes or eggs Benedict with hash browns.

Being friends with restaurant people is fantastic, but it can come at a cost that I think might be controversial: You have to take the good with the bad. In other words, if you're not getting the perks you normally get—or even if the service is outright terrible—you're not allowed to say anything about it.

I'm dead serious. You don't complain. Not to the server, not to the manager, not to the owner, the hostess, or even the goddamn bathroom attendant.

Just keep your mouth shut. Get over it.

It happens. People have bad days. You have to realize that you're in a privileged position. You're a regular. Ninety-nine times out of a hundred, you're getting service that the normies would kill for. You're getting extras that the richest guy in the room couldn't get even if he started tipping with $100 bills.

So shut it.

Everyone has an off night. The best restaurant in the world, the most skilled server, the most talented chef—they're gonna screw up at their job every now and again. Just shake it off, tip like you normally would, and trust that it's going to be better next time.

And if it isn't better next time? Or the time after that? Well, that might be your sign to become a regular elsewhere.

As much as I love small, intimate meals with just myself or my wife, restaurants certainly appreciate it when you bring more people. From a short-term business perspective, obviously the more diners, the bigger the bill. But also thinking long-term, the more new people that you, as a regular, can introduce to a place the better. Your evangelizing for the restaurant does more to put future butts in seats than their entire marketing department can ever hope to.

Your local haunt will also appreciate it if you think of them when you're doing larger events—birthdays, anniversaries, business meetings, and so on. Even if it's not the type of venue that normally does large-scale gatherings, they can usually accommodate you if you ask. And as a regular you can be assured that not only will they take good care of you and your party, but they will go above and beyond to make sure the night is a success.

My high-flying Manhattan days are mostly over. I'm a married man and I've left the big city behind for life in small-town Connecticut. But that doesn't mean that I still don't have my spot. It's not as flashy as Wolfgang's, or as sceney as Toro, but my wife and I love the local brewpub. They don't have foie gras like Rebelle, but they do have Mexican Mondays with some of the best Tex-Mex cuisine in the county.

We like to sit with our favorite bartender, Danielle, and just dish about small town gossip. Or we'll yuck it up with the locals—the same locals, I might add, who hated us when we first moved to town. They called us "Citiots"! But we won them over too.

Instead of wining and dining business associates, or closing out the bar in the wee hours of the morning, I'm just using the place as my college football hangout. Every Saturday my wife drops me off and I sit with Collin the bartender and we watch all the games. Collin and I trade quips, making fun of teams, coaches, and fans that we see on TV. And the perks are still there—he'll comp me a drink or two—but it's not even about the perks at this point. We genuinely enjoy one another's company. We truly know each other. He's quick to bring me the scotch I like, or mineral water, or to ask how my dogs are doing. I chat with him about his kids. We share personal stuff.

It's the same whether you are at the fanciest of restaurants or the most salt-of-the-earth local establishment: food and hospitality is about shared culture, and the real value isn't always in what you're being served but in the friendships made under those roofs.

I've been ushered through crowds of waiting diners in Manhattan's temples of meat. I've been escorted through kitchens (I swear to God, exactly like that scene in *Goodfellas!*) to get to the front of restaurants. I've been allowed to park for free in roped-off areas where people pay an arm and a leg for parking. All of this just goes to show that my formula works. My philosophy is the real deal, and you can make it work for yourself too if you just follow the cardinal rule: don't act like an asshole!

Be kind, be funny, and be genuinely interested in the lives of the people who are waiting on you, and I guarantee you that good things will follow.

Chapter 6
THE HOUSE THAT SHRIMP BUILT

TRUE STORY: MY father once asked my mother if he could install giant statues of shrimp in our front yard.

Normal families put in a tasteful bird bath, or some rose bushes or something. Maybe a garden gnome or a Virgin Mary statue.

Not the Riccas.

No, we had to do something *weird*.

But what better way to honor the cheeky little crustacean who was almost single-handedly responsible for the family's good fortune? Or so my dad argued.

Luckily for the neighbors, he was overruled by my ever-prudent mother. She put her foot down as hard as I'd ever seen her do it.

I'm still not sure to this day if my dad was entirely serious or not, but the fact that he even considered it shows you how important this creature was—and still is—to Val's Ocean Pacific.

Shrimp is the most popular seafood in America, by a long shot. Your average American will eat about nineteen pounds of seafood a year, and almost five pounds of that is shrimp. (Compare that to three pounds of salmon, two pounds of canned tuna, and less than one pound of everything else.)

A shrimp is a crustacean. It's the same family as lobsters, crabs, and crayfish. Similar flavor and texture too. But it's way more popular than any of those alternatives for a couple of reasons. For one, it's a lot easier to eat. Just look at the implements they give you for your average crab or lobster dinner: all sorts of medieval-looking tools to crack and gouge and pound the meat from the tough shells. Shrimp, on the other hand, can just be gently peeled with your fingers.

The real reason shrimp is so ubiquitous, though? It's cheap, relatively speaking. And thanks to careful management and large farming operations, the price is stable year round. Even during COVID, when we saw the price of other crustaceans go through the roof—king crab, snow crab, and lobster all doubled or even tripled in price—shrimp stayed about the same.

It wasn't always this way, of course. Up until the late seventies, the majority of shrimp was wild-caught and heavily dependent on the seasons and location. This made it as difficult to obtain as lobster and crab, and accordingly just as expensive to buy. While there were some attempts to breed and raise shrimp in captivity, the animal was finicky, and farm-raised shrimp were almost as difficult to produce and expensive to buy as the wild stuff. Unless you were lucky enough to live on the Louisiana coast, or privileged enough to regularly dine at white table-cloth restaurants, you probably rarely got to taste shrimp.

Then in the eighties—serendipitously around the same time that my dad was setting off on his own business venture—aquaculture scientists figured their shit out. They developed the technology to raise plump, healthy shrimp, in captivity, year round. And the industry exploded. The US market got flooded with inexpensive, foreign-farmed shrimp.

In many ways, this was a good thing. Shrimp became a more democratic food. There's no way that Red Lobster's all-you-can-eat shrimp extravaganza or Popeye's popcorn shrimp value meal could even exist without farmed shrimp. (Interestingly enough, the relatively inexpensive farmed shrimp that Red Lobster uses is superior to the product that a lot of pricey, fancy, white tablecloth restaurants often ask me to get for them.)

In some other ways, however, this was a bad thing. Because in the middle of the crustacean gold rush (pink rush?) there were, of course, some bad actors just looking to cash in on the trend, and some truly heinous product started circulating.

When my dad started his business, it was a very different time in the restaurant industry. Most owners and chefs cared deeply about quality. It was a badge of honor to use the best product, even if that cut into the profit margin.

And that attitude was found in every facet of the business, from your temples of fine dining all the way down to the lowliest corner Chinese joint. Everyone used the best of the best.

But as time went on, as Americans started to cook at home less and less, more restaurants sprouted up to fill the country's growing demand for prepared meals. As the competition grew for customers, restaurateurs began to care less about quality and focused ever more on pricing. That's the attitude that the purveyors of the worst shrimp are taking advantage of.

Before we go on, let me tell you about what a shrimp *should* be like. The platonic ideal for shrimp is wild caught. A top-of-the-line farmed shrimp can still be pretty good, don't get me wrong. But when the shrimp grow naturally, everything about them is better—the flavor will be more complex. It will taste briny, like the ocean, but still delicate. The texture will be firm, and not rubbery. Wild shrimp take to the heat better, too, cooking faster and more predictably.

A wild shrimp will have a distinct color to it, also. This color varies—it can be brown, or pink, or grey. But never pale-verging-on-translucent, which is the case with a lot of farmed shrimp. (There's one exception to this color rule—there's a very rare type of wild-caught Hawaiian shrimp that's also pale and translucent. But odds are you'll never encounter this on the mainland. It's a rare enough product that it seldom is sold outside its natural environment.)

The reason for the disparity between wild and farmed is that even in the best, highest-quality environments, farmed shrimp is still a somewhat unnatural product. The pools where they are raised limit their movement, so their meat develops differently. Their diet is tightly regulated. Their water is flooded with various antibiotics to stave off illness, and chemicals to control PH-levels and algae growth.

Even without the heavy use of the various soaks and brines that suppliers use to plump up their product for market, farm-raised shrimp will always taste a little blander than their wild counterpart. And if they are heavily treated with chemicals, which is sometimes unfortunately the case, they can have a confusing flavor profile. When a shrimp is overly-chemicalized, it might not cook properly in the pan, or take a long time to brown. When you taste them after cooking, they might still give you the impression that they're raw. At worst, they can leave an odd aftertaste.

I'm generally the shrimp taster here at the office because I am super-sensitive to chemicals. The way you can detect chemicals is after you eat the shrimp there's a residue in your mouth. Sort of an extra level of sliminess in your saliva, and slipperiness on your tongue. A few minutes after eating you feel the urge to chug a ton of water. That is a clear indication that your shrimp have been chemicalized or that you are consuming a lower grade product than you'd like.

There's still a home in the industry for farm-raised shrimp. Like I said earlier, it made this once-exotic food accessible to the masses. Another argument in favor of farmed is that in many of the most popular preparations that people (especially Americans) enjoy, it's not necessary to get the absolute top-tier product. If you're just going to batter, deep fry, and douse some shrimp in buffalo sauce, you don't need the best of the best.

Another reason is consistency.

Let me explain: for my money, the absolute best-tasting shrimp in the world is a Mexican brown shrimp. They have the best flavor of anything on the market, and a firm, meaty texture. It's the shrimp that I bring home with me nine times out of ten when I'm cooking for myself.

But they're not desired in the restaurant world. Almost no chef will let these into his or her kitchen, because they're kind of a pain in the ass to deal with. Like all wild shrimp, they're only available at certain times of the year, and the fact that there's a limited market for them in the States makes them even harder to source consistently. They come in somewhat irregular, non-uniform sizes. They tend to swim deep and eat a varied diet, which makes the vein that runs up their backside large and quite dirty. That means that a kitchen wanting to serve them will need a bit more time and labor in the kitchen to clean them (or "de-turd" them, as David Spade put it so memorably in *Tommy Boy*).

So even though they have the best flavor, hands down, they're always going to get outsold by farm-raised shrimp, which is cheaper, available year-round, more uniform in size, and less filled with . . . well, poop.

That's not to say that nobody wants the wild stuff. Wild shrimp is still the best, and there are a lot of restaurants that insist on having only the best. Some chefs prefer my beloved Mexican browns, and will accept no substitute. We're more than happy to provide it to them.

Wild Mexican *white* shrimp is the type that's the most in demand. That product hits a sweet spot on price, quality, availability, and consistency. If that's not available, shrimp from Panama and Ecuador is also desired. Domestic shrimp can be pretty good, but we sell a lot less of it than you'd expect, mostly due to pricing concerns: the relatively high labor costs from American producers drive the price up.

Even after a restaurant settles on a country of origin for their shrimp, there's still another subcategory they have to deal with: all shrimp are graded and sorted by number. A #1 wild white is the best. Uniform in size, appearance, and hardness of shell. A #2 is what you might call "irregular." Maybe the shell's a little soft, or the sizes within the batch vary a lot. It still tastes good, but the presentation suffers, and depending on what kind of restaurant you have, that might be important to you.

Another popular type of shrimp that you've probably seen by name on menus somewhere is black tiger shrimp. Steakhouses and chain restaurants love these, because they generally come in large sizes, and look fantastic with grill marks, sitting on a plate next to a giant slab of beef. The tiger shrimps that make it to the United States are generally farmed, and the best version of those come from Vietnam. The next most desirable countries of origin are Indonesia, India, Thailand, the Philippines, and Malaysia, in that order.

Continuing down the hierarchy of shrimp, we have the vannamei variety. These are an incredibly cheap variety to farm, so you see operations cropping up all over the globe. This type in particular is where you start to see sketchy product sneak into the supply chain. Vannameis are often passed off as higher-end varieties, and it's hard for even seasoned chefs to tell the difference sometimes, let alone diners.

The bottom of the barrel is pre-peeled and de-veined shrimp. These are usually vannameis, but can come in all kinds of varieties. There was a time that restaurants would avoid this product like the plague, and for a good reason—there's no way to know what kind of quality you're getting.

Ideally, when any shrimp comes to me, it's going to be shell-on, flash frozen on the same boat it was caught on, or at least as humanly close to the time it was caught as possible. But when a producer takes the time to peel the shrimp themselves, by definition you're extending the amount of time between the shrimp coming out of the water and the shrimp going into deep freeze. Is that time a few hours? Is it a few days? Or *weeks*, even? There's just no telling how long that product sat around a warehouse, waiting to be processed, or how many preservative chemicals were added to keep it from spoiling in the meantime.

(A producer once told me that he'd visited a processing plant in the mountains of South America, where shrimp were being pre-peeled and frozen. The shrimp made their long journey from the ocean to the plant in the back of a pick-up truck. Not a refrigerated truck, mind you—an open-bed pickup. They were just taken off the fishing boats, piled into burlap sacks, tossed in the truck bed, and driven four hours to the plant.)

When you order a case of pre-peeled, you're really rolling the dice. But restaurants still do it, because it's cheaper, and it saves them time and labor. I do my best to make sure that any cases that pass through my warehouse are as good as they can possibly be, but there's only so much I can do.

Adding to the confusion are the various names for sizing. Terms like "jumbo," "colossal," and "extra small" are tossed around, but these can mean different things to different people. It's much better to go by the numbering scheme, which is based on how many shrimp typically add up to a pound. The lower the number, the larger the shrimp. For example, 16/20 is a pretty decent-sized shrimp, meaning they're big enough that that a pound will usually have between 16 and 20. If you want to go smaller, there's 21/25 all the way down to 71/90. If you want to go super large, you're looking at a U12, or even a U8.

With all of the different types of shrimp, sizes, countries of origin, wild vs. farmed, and so on, it becomes easy to see why restaurants might get confused, and why there's a lot of room for unscrupulous people to take advantage of them. Mislabeling is rampant, as is outright fraud. And the stakes are high. The incentives to cheat are all there. Wild Mexican white shrimp, for example, can be $2–4 per pound more expensive than its counterpart from Panama or Ecuador. In a fifty-pound case, that translates to a $100-$200 difference.

Even if you're certain about the country of origin, the price differences still abound. Wild #1 is $4 per pound more than wild #2, and it's not necessarily easy to tell the difference with the naked eye. Farmed is $3–4 per pound cheaper than wild, and once again, good luck telling the two apart if you don't know what you're looking for!

ONE GUY WHO always knows what he's looking for is Val Ricca.
My father didn't let my mother's firm rejection of his lawn decor prevent him from spreading his shrimp knowledge to anyone who would listen. He made it his personal mission to evangelize for the tiny delicious creatures, and to this day whenever I picture him at a social event at someone's home, I see him in the kitchen, holding court above a sinkful of shrimp. The gathered crowd would listen as he explained the pros and cons of Mexican versus domestic shrimp, or watch as he demonstrated the proper way to defrost and peel them.

"Don't microwave them. Don't put them in a warm tub of water, either. You don't want to accidentally cook them! Just put them in the sink, with a light trickle of room temperature water constantly running. Light is the key. You don't want it to be so strong that it bruises the shells." (You'd be surprised how many restaurants don't follow these simple directives, but in a hectic kitchen they're often pressed for time and flying by the seat of their pants. I've lost count of the number of times chefs have called me complaining that I passed them bad product, only for it to come out during the conversation that they'd done a quickie defrost by dunking an entire case of frozen shrimp in hot water.)

With shrimp established as his calling card, my father was determined to never show up for a social event without some shrimp in tow. Usually this involved him prepping a dish at home and driving it a short distance, or tossing some frozen ones in a cooler. But every now and again he'd bring his payload on longer journeys.

The entire extended Ricca clan had a tradition of doing an annual spring trip to Anna Maria Island in Florida. Despite its location on the Gulf of Mexico, not far from the Louisiana coast (a.k.a. one of the best shrimping grounds in the world), my dad didn't have confidence that he'd be able to get his hands on some local product that was up to his standards. He was feeding his own relatives, so having the absolute best was paramount.

His solution was to bring the shrimp onto the plane with him, something he did for many years without incident. There was one year it didn't quite go as planned, though.

The morning we were scheduled to depart, there he was in our kitchen with a giant block of frozen shrimp, wrapping it in aluminum foil. He plopped it in a Styrofoam cooler, dragged it through security at JFK (this was pre-9/11, so it didn't cause much of a stir) and onto the plane, where he hoisted the whole thing into an overhead bin.

An hour into the flight, the guy sitting in the aisle seat behind us rang for the flight attendant, and complained that there was something dripping on him from the air vent—*and it smelled like fish.*

My dad was probably lucky that they didn't have air marshals back then, because he would have definitely been detained on suspicion of seafood-related terrorism. As it was, he got off easy, offering a heartfelt apology and a promise to send the injured party a case of lobster tails. He and my mother still crack up about it to this day, the time a leaky disposable cooler almost led to an air rage incident.

Now that my old man is semi-retired, I hope to pick up his mantle as the King of Shrimp. It's going to be tough to fill those shoes. He has deep knowledge not only of everything that moves through our warehouse, but is an expert on how each type will react to the customer's preferred cooking method, and how it will interact with the other ingredients.

If he's dealing with a Spanish restaurant, for example, he'll tell them their best bet is pink shrimp from "BG." (That's British Guiana, which is what Guyana used to be known as until 1966. But the industry is very slow to move on from old familiar nomenclature.) The reason BG pink is perfect for Spanish joints is that it takes really well to garlic and olive oil, the main ingredients in the insanely tasty dish camarones al ajillo. This simple dish lets the ingredients speak for themselves, and there's nothing like it when a chef bathes the shrimp in a delicious shower of garlic and oil, and brings it to your table piping-hot and still bubbling.

This kind of personalization—knowing and anticipating a customer's needs better than they themselves can do it—is what makes my father the King of Shrimp. I'm getting close, but for now I'm still just the Prince of Prawns.

A side note—there's a lot of confusion about shrimp vs. prawns. The scientific difference is that shrimp live in saltwater and prawns are in fresh. But in practice, the word gets pretty muddled. On my side of the industry, there's a tendency to call anything that's on the larger side a "prawn." And on the restaurant side, they'll sometimes use the term to denote a shrimp that's served with the head on, or just to make a dish sound even more classy or exotic. Adding to the confusion, in the UK and certain other locales, "prawn" is just their word for all shrimp. Ultimately, all you need to know is that prawns are a little bit milder in taste than shrimp, but the two can be used interchangeably in most recipes.

Okay, side note over—let's talk about how I'm preparing to take over the throne.

My long journey to the top started with rock shrimp.

You've definitely seen them on menus before. They're wildly desirable little suckers from Florida. They got their name because of how hard their shells are, which makes them notoriously difficult to clean. They're also extremely seasonal. All that means they're expensive, of course. But they taste like tiny lobsters, and people love them, so certain restaurants must have them.

About a decade ago, chefs were begging me for these guys all the time, and I fulfilled what orders I could, but like I said—they're very seasonal. Now, I try to be practical in this business, and a lot of my time is spent dealing with people who want the latest trendy ingredient. But when restaurants ask me for something like that, I try to read between the lines and figure out what they're really asking for. Their mouths may be saying "rock shrimp", but when I investigate further and ask what they're planning to do with the product, I discover that the application they're thinking of may not be best suited to the ingredient. You have to be nimble and creative sometimes to fulfill the needs of your clients.

So I noted all the people asking me for rock shrimp, explained the difficulty and expense involved, and offered a substitute in its place: one of my suppliers in Argentina had recently sent along some beautiful wild red shrimp. Like the rock shrimp, they had a gorgeous blush color, plus a taste and texture similar to lobster. *Unlike* the rock shrimp, they were available year round and reasonably priced. It took some wheedling on my part, but I got a bunch of my customers that were looking for rock shrimp to switch over to the Argentinean. I kept pushing, and the product eventually caught on.

Soon, other restaurants that had never before asked me for rock shrimp figured out that there was this new thing on the scene, and they started asking for the Argentinean red as well. No one else in New York had these. I was the only guy. And I had created this market out of thin air.

Here's the weird thing, though. I noticed a lot of the restaurants that were happily serving the product from Argentina were still listing it on their menu as Florida rock shrimp. The brand name—the cachet—of Florida rock shrimp was still winning out. That's pretty typical, and I didn't take offense. I did, however, find it offensive that they weren't lowering the prices that they charged their diners for "rock shrimp," when I was giving the restaurants Argentinean red for a fraction of the price. Again, this was typical. I didn't particularly like it, but you should know by this point in the book that it's just something that happens.

Meanwhile, word eventually got back to Argentina that the Americans were *loco* for the *camarones rojas*, and there was money to be made. So where there used to be a handful of suppliers that were only dealing with me, suddenly there were dozens of new guys, and they were selling to everybody. The market that I had invented was suddenly flooded, as all my competitors got their own hookups.

And guess what? The quality of the product plummeted. It became harder and harder to get the good ones, and we started seeing product that was mistreated, just caked in chemicals. Some of these shrimps were so artificially plumped and processed that they'd shrink down two or three sizes when you cooked them!

When the restaurants figured out they could no longer rely on Argentina to supply them with their faux-Florida rock shrimp, they went off in a dozen different directions. Some of them—the reputable venues—went back to the OG product, putting it on the menu as the seasons allowed. Others went in the opposite direction, subbing in whatever they could get their hands on, including the dreaded pre-peeled and de-veined of miscellaneous origin.

Today, people have started to come to me for shrimp advice, just like they used to come to my dad. I don't yet have all the knowledge that he does, but there are a few things that I'm happy to pass along to anyone who asks.

One of those pieces of advice I'm very confident to give, because I learned it myself through a hard-won lesson: Beware of the rock shrimp.

Chapter 7
WHITE TABLECLOTHS, BLACK HEARTS

I LIKE A "nice" restaurant as much as the next guy. It's a great feeling to go out somewhere with a lively atmosphere, cool music, and beautiful people. A place where the employees are trained to kiss your ass—not because you're a regular, but because they assume that by eating there, you are by definition a well-off individual who will leave them a large tip.

But when it comes to the quality of the food, there's no worse deal in the entire industry than a fancy restaurant.

There are exceptions to the rule, of course. The fanciest of the fancy—places like Manhattan's Le Bernardin, or Jean Georges or Per Se—are actually the total package. Attentive service, an atmosphere that just reeks of money and taste, and food that is thoughtfully sourced and meticulously prepared. But elite institutions like this are rare, and intentionally priced out of reach of the average consumer. These are dining destinations that will cost you $125 and up per head just to get in the door. Add in wine and cocktails, or a ten-course chef's tasting menu, and you're easily looking at a tab that could top $300 to $400 per person.

Is that experience worth it? A lot of people think so, as reservations on that top tier are perennially completely booked months in advance.

I don't really have a quibble with those types of restaurants. Chefs like Eric Ripert, Jean-Georges Vongerichten, and Thomas Keller are talented and definitely know what to do with a good piece of seafood.

My problem is with the tier of restaurants immediately beneath it—restaurants that your average diner would still consider "fancy."

Living in New York, I have a lot of friends who frequent these types of places. Often the friends are about as fancy as the restaurants. They have fancy jobs (usually in law or finance) and fancy degrees from fancy schools. Fancy upbringings in Greenwich, Connecticut or Boston or one of the ritzy Chicago suburbs.

But being raised around money, or working in an industry solely devoted to moving money around, doesn't necessarily mean you have a clue about food. I find that more often the opposite is true. These are not discerning consumers. And there's a whole industry in New York devoted to exploiting their lack of knowledge and taste.

Remember earlier when I talked about the restaurant where Kanye West was being served subpar shrimp? That's the type of place I'm talking about. These restaurants project an image that they are offering you the best experience, but it's built entirely on a bed of lies. Trendy locations, a cool Spotify playlist in the dining room, and all the reclaimed wood and Edison bulbs in the world can't obscure the fact that the food they're serving is shit. But 99 percent of the people who eat there will never know that. They've fallen for the smoke and mirrors.

They're not going to dinner—they're going to a second-rate magic show. And they're paying $40 to $50 per entree for the experience.

So how do the restaurants get away with this? Let's look at a few of the ways.

BUZZWORDS

We've talked quite a bit about how your menu is lying to you. Fancy restaurants are the kings of this, liberally sprinkling their menu with trendy ingredients and buzzwords that sound good, but are essentially meaningless when it comes to flavor or quality. It's marketing, specifically concocted to dress up cheap ingredients and make them sound like something special.

Let's take a place like Nobu, as an example. The restaurant was opened in the mid-nineties by Japanese chef Nobu Matsuhisa and a few partners, including Robert De Niro. Yes, *that* Robert De Niro. (Apparently he was a fan of Matsuhisa's Los Angeles restaurant, and spent years convincing the chef to bring his talents to De Niro's lower Manhattan neighborhood of Tribeca.)

The restaurant was immediately successful. Some of that was surely due to De Niro's star power and connections. A lot more of it was thanks to timing—they were lucky to not only be in a neighborhood that was up-and-coming and would soon rise to heights right out of the wet dreams of real estate brokers, but also managed to get in basically on the ground floor of sushi's popularity in America.

Nobu's success had at least one more element behind it: the black cod.

Nobu's signature dish was—and is to this day—a fillet of black cod, marinated in miso and sake. Now I've had the dish. I'm not gonna lie: it's good. Black cod is a delicious fish, oily and buttery and rich with a tasty skin. And Nobu is a talented chef. The flavors of his marinade give the fish a salty, savory sweetness that is undeniably delicious.

But at the time of this writing, the price on the dish is a hefty $46. This might sound okay to some of you. "Allen," you might say, "this is a world-class restaurant, serving a rare and exotic fish. $46 isn't so bad."

Let's pump the brakes for a second.

What you don't know is that "black cod" is hiding a dirty little secret. That's right—move over, "Chilean sea bass." We've got another classic seafood rebranding on our hands!

In the industry, the "black cod" is known by its more common name: sablefish. It's always been a tasty fish, but it wasn't necessarily a popular one until Nobu renamed it and started slinging it to investment bankers and entertainment types. And the funny thing about it is that while the price has gone up a little along with its popularity, it's still not a particularly rare or exotic fish, so it's not expensive at all. Tuna, swordfish, and scallops are all much pricier purchases. But they don't have the manufactured cachet of "black cod," so they're a much tougher sell at $46.

The irony is that if you walk a few avenues west from Tribeca to Chinatown, you'll find sablefish on dozens of menus. It'll be a huge portion, unlike Nobu's dainty fillet, and it's only going to cost you $12 or $13. So that's an extra $33 or so you're paying, for what? To rub elbows with Howard Stern or one of the Kardashians?

Nobu's fortune was built on the foundation of taking a relatively inexpensive fish, renaming it, classing it up, and serving it to people who don't know any better. And credit where credit is due—the racket worked like a charm. As of 2021, the Nobu empire now spans forty-eight different locations across the globe, plus twenty-one hotels.

Not bad for a lowly little sablefish.

EXCLUSIVITY

Another hallmark of the fancy restaurant is artificial exclusivity. They want to give the impression that people are absolutely breaking down the doors to get in. Sometimes this is actually true. But often, especially when a restaurant is new, or trying to make a name for itself, this is a blatant lie.

Sometimes you'll call a place for a reservation, and they'll tell you they have nothing available. *Fine*, you think. *They're popular. I'm not surprised they're busy.* But you decide to go there anyway, try your luck as a walk-in. And when you get there you discover that the place is a quarter full at 8:00 on a Friday night.

At that point you might be thinking, *Jackpot! It looks like a dozen people canceled their reservations*! So you ask the hostess to seat you. "We can't," she says. "We're fully booked." You pointedly look around the restaurant, while the hostess suggests you sit at the bar.

Now eating at the bar isn't so bad. Sometimes I prefer it! Especially when eating alone, or with just one other person. The vibe at the bar is decidedly different from the dining room, and that can be fun. But certain restaurants or cuisines just aren't conducive to bar eating, and a table would be better. But you decide to tough it out anyway, because you really do want to try the food. So you proceed to go with the flow and eat your dinner perched on a stool.

Ultimately, you're there for an hour or more, and does that dining room fill up in the meantime? It sure as shit doesn't! A few stragglers wander in and take their tables, but the majority of them remain empty. Sometimes, insultingly, they even have little signs on them that say "Reserved."

Why do restaurants do this? It's sort of a "fake it til you make it" attitude. The joint knows that it isn't popular yet, but it has aspirations to be a trendy dining destination. So they lie and say they're full, all the time. The hope is that eventually word gets around that it's one of the toughest seats in town, and diners start to believe the hype. If it's that hard to get into, they must be doing something good, right?

I love my city, but I have to admit that New Yorkers are especially susceptible to this psychological jujitsu. They are constantly on the lookout for what's hot and what's next. Plus, in a town where most people don't own a car, we've had to come up with alternative status signifiers, and hard-to-get restaurant reservations are one of those signifiers that we've settled on.

SEX APPEAL

Have you ever walked into a restaurant and did a double-take, thinking you'd accidentally walked onto a movie set or a modeling shoot? At some restaurants, every employee —from the hostess in the slinky dress, to the muscular, tattooed bartender, to the willowy servers that glide through the dining room, all the way down to the busboys in tight t-shirts with dreamy eyes—is absolutely gorgeous.

This is no accident. This is a conscious choice that some restaurateurs make. They want to project a sense of luxury and glamor in all aspects of their business, and once they've tackled the signage and the dining room decor and the dishwater and the menu, the final frontier is the employees. Hot workers equal hot restaurant, or so the thinking goes.

I know about this practice from very personal experience. My wife, who is the most gorgeous woman I've ever seen, spoken to, met, or even thought about (*she's standing over my shoulder as I write this sentence . . . please send help*) was a hostess. That's how we met, in fact. It turned out that she was a very good hostess, but that's not why the restaurant initially hired her, an aspiring artist with admittedly zero restaurant experience. No, they hired her because they wanted a young, cute, tattooed brunette greeting customers. They figured that a pretty face would make the customers feel extra welcome. And it worked on a lot of diners. None more so than me!

But it hardly seems fair. Attractive people already have a lot of privileges in life. It's already way easier for them to find clothes that look good on them, gain Instagram followers, get babies to smile at them, and—obviously—convince people to go to bed with them. Should it also be easier for them to get hired?

It feels like it should be illegal to hire based on looks, but it is decidedly not. When hiring for a restaurant, (or any other business—remember what Abercrombie & Fitch employees looked like in the nineties?) employers are 100 percent allowed to screen for looks.

People often don't believe me when I tell them this. It sounds made up. But owners would argue that the appearance of their staff—the people who interact with customers—is an important part of their business, and they should have the ability to control it. And that's not just for restaurants. That's for every industry. That's why a fashion designer doesn't have to hire a model if he doesn't like the way she looks. That's why your office job is allowed to tell you what to wear. A dress code is just another form of appearance discrimination, when you think about it.

The bottom line is that "attractiveness" is not a legally-protected attribute when it comes to hiring. Age, race, religion, disabilities—those are all protected attributes. A restaurant owner can't post a job listing that says "no Jews" but he can definitely post one saying "no uggos."

It feels ethically dubious, and honestly just plain icky, but it's not illegal. A restaurateur is pretty much in the clear to staff a restaurant in the same way that he'd cast a porno, and many of them do.

HIRED CELEBRITY DINERS

I've talked a bit about the intersection of the celebrity world and the culinary world, so it probably won't surprise you when I tell you sometimes the relationship is a lot more transactional than anyone realizes.

That's right—restaurants are paying celebrities to eat.

Sometimes the payment merely comes in the form of a comped meal. But often enough there's not only free food and booze included in the deal, but cash changing hands as well.

The benefits for the celebrity are obvious. After all, that heavily marked-up fish goes down a lot easier when you know you're not going to be paying for it at the end of the night. But the restaurant benefits as well. Especially with up-and-coming establishments that are trying to cement their status as a "hotspot," what better way to drum up some interest than having paparazzi camped on the sidewalk hoping for a shot of Rihanna exiting the premises?

Tabloids and gossip sites are only too happy to play along. They'll run the photos and do a short blurb where a "source" or an "insider" or a "spy" or a "tipster" (all of those are just code words for "hired publicist") will breathlessly give details like: Who was the celebrity with? What did the celebrity order? What were they wearing? What kind of mood were they in? Did they leave a big tip?

These types of stories also serve a valuable purpose for the dining public—they let us know which restaurants to avoid in the near future, as any ensuing bump in popularity all but assures a swarm of annoying celeb chasers will clamor to get in for several weeks after. And once a restaurant achieves that critical mass of buzz and popularity, that gives them license to let the quality of their ingredients slip, potentially ruining the place forever.

THOSE ARE JUST a few of the smoke-and-mirrors tricks that certain restaurants use to fill seats. It's not really offensive to me. I totally get it, and I don't blame them for what they do. But I do have to laugh that a lot of restaurant owners, when faced with the choice of improving their PR or improving their food, so often choose the former.

So my last word of advice on this topic is that while you should go to these restaurants with a bit of caution, and approach them with some skepticism, it's still okay to go to them once in a while. If your idea of a good night out is to drink some $15 cocktails, have a mediocre $39 entree, and ogle some servers, then I'm not going to tell you how to live your life.

But just know that there's much better food out there.

And later on, I'm going to tell you how to find it.

Chapter 8
THE PINK PLAGUE

FULL DISCLOSURE BEFORE we begin this chapter in earnest—I can't fucking stand salmon.

Seems weird for a fish guy to say, right? Especially about the second most popular seafood item in the United States.

That's right—Americans are salmon-crazy. And it's a relatively recent phenomenon, too. It's only in the past ten years or so that salmon surpassed tuna on the list of per capita consumption. (My friends in the shrimp kingdom, of course, remain number one with a bullet.)

But I really do hate those ugly fuckers. And they are ugly. If you don't believe me, do a Google image search right now for "sockeye salmon." That's some nightmare fuel right there.

If you are one of those salmon-lovers, I don't blame you. Its popularity isn't hard to decode. It's a versatile fish that responds nicely to almost any cooking style.

Grilled? Sure.

Sautéed? Why not.

Baked? Beautiful.

Steamed. Broiled. Tartared. Ceviched. Smoked. Cured. Sashimied.

You name it, salmon can do it, coming through consistently with a mild flavor and nice texture. And it's forgiving, too. The high fat content means that it's very difficult to overcook. Chefs love it for this reason, as do caterers (how many weddings have you been to where the fish choice is salmon?), and home cooks who would normally never go anywhere near a fish will still break out the salmon fillets on occasion.

So yeah, I don't blame you if you do like it. I don't think you're a rube or anything, or someone with bad taste. My dislike of the fish is entirely personal, and rooted in childhood trauma.

I must have been fourteen or fifteen years old when I went with my dad to a Lower East Side restaurant that shall remain nameless. We were there to try a special tasting menu, and the salmon just didn't look right to me. I tried it, and it didn't taste right either. But I didn't know as much back then, and I didn't want to be rude to the chef, or look unsophisticated, so I made a show of eating a big portion.

I should have noticed that my dad wasn't really eating his. And to be fair, he should have warned me to hold back. Either way, we both paid for it on the car ride back home, with him having to stop the car every few miles so I could hop out and projectile vomit onto the side of the road.

I've barely touched salmon since.

It's funny, because I'm in a decidedly pro-salmon business—we sell somewhere in the range of eight to ten thousand pounds of it a week— as well as a pro-salmon household: my wife loves it.

Just the other week, she was craving a piece of it, and suggested that we cook it for dinner. I told her to knock herself out, as long as she got me a ribeye steak in the process. So she went to the grocery store and picked up a fillet of regular old skin-on farmed Atlantic salmon. When she got home I caught a glimpse at the receipt. She'd paid $19.99 a pound for it! That's for a fish that I know the grocery had snagged for $7.50 a pound, tops. That's a pretty outrageous markup, and one of the many reasons why I advise people to never shop for fish at a grocery store (more on that later).

But it also got me thinking. Salmon is a fish that's ripe for exactly that sort of abuse. The second-most-popular seafood in the country is, in a weird way, a victim of its own success. And as ubiquitous as it is, the people who buy it, prepare it, and eat it know almost nothing about it.

LET'S TALK ABOUT wild salmon versus farmed salmon.

If I offered you a choice between the two, you'd say "Allen, of course I want the wild stuff. That's better."

And I'd shoot right back: "No, you don't. That's not what you want. You think that's what you want, but you really don't."

As someone who has had to accept the returns of hundreds of cases of wild salmon from confused or disappointed restaurants, trust me when I say that when you ask for wild salmon, you're not getting what you expect.

Let me explain: I'm going to ask you to close your eyes and think of a salmon fillet. What do you see? I'm going to guess it's pinkish-orange, with thick white lines running throughout.

Is that right?

If that's what you're picturing, that's farmed salmon.

That trademark color, and those striations in the flesh? That's something you see in farmed salmon, and *only* in farmed salmon. Wild salmon looks completely different. It's always less fatty, so instead of thick white lines you get thin ones, or none at all. And that trademark "salmon" color is completely different in wild specimens. Sometimes it's a much deeper orange, verging on red, with the flesh looking closer to bluefin tuna than what we think of as the "classic" salmon. Or sometimes it's much lighter, too, with some less saturated oranges, and some shades that are just barely pink. It varies by species, location, season, diet, and so on.

And there's even a needle-in-a-haystack salmon that's pure white.

This elusive creature is a king salmon (also known as a chinook). It's one of the fattiest wild salmon, and we all know that fat equals delicious, so they're sought-after fish, and have a price tag to match. Nineteen out of twenty chinooks have deep orangey-red flesh, but that last one out of twenty has a genetic defect that causes it to process its diet differently, and develop light white-colored muscles. Aficionados swear that the white meat is even fattier, oilier ,and more delicious than the common king salmon, so these "ivory kings" command a premium price.

The crazy thing is all the chinooks look identical on the outside, so the only way to find out if you've landed a prized white one is to slice into it.

Anyway, the point of all this is to say that wild salmon are susceptible to all kinds of variation. You could say that makes for a far more interesting fish, but people in the restaurant business don't necessarily want "interesting." They, and their customers, want consistency. Consistency means that a fish is available year round, and when it's placed in front of the diner, it should look exactly like what they expect. Hence the popularity of farmed salmon.

Is farmed salmon "better" than wild? Most aficionados would say no, wild is better. It has more interesting, more complex, deeper flavor. But the vast majority of the public, when given a choice in a side-by-side tasting, will instead choose the farmed. They'll even go so far as to say they *hate* the taste of the wild. "That doesn't even taste like salmon," they'll say. And they're right, in a way—farmed salmon is the flavor that people are used to, so wild salmon tastes completely unfamiliar to them.

Think of it like the difference between chicken and duck. Most gourmands would swear that duck is a "better," richer, and more interesting food. But chicken is what people are used to, and is orders of magnitude more popular. (Consider that the average American eats about one-third pound of duck a year, compared to more than ninety-seven pounds of chicken.)

Farmed salmon has a few other legs (fins?) up on its wild counterpart. Like those aforementioned fatty white striations that run through the flesh—they insulate farmed salmon from the heat of cooking, causing it to flake beautifully when finished. That's an advantage over wild salmon's relative lack of these striations. And that's entirely a result of the farmed salmon being fattened up for the market, like any other livestock. Throughout their life, and especially in the weeks before harvesting, they're fed a diet of—well, you can never be sure—but it sometimes includes corn and soy, just like they'd give to any steer or pig in the weeks before the slaughterhouse. It also sometimes includes a ground fish slurry, which I'm guessing is much tastier for the salmon than it sounds to us.

Canadian salmon is the most popular farmed type I sell. The supply chain in the Great White North is by far the most trustworthy. You know the provenance, you know the suppliers, and you know that they treated their scaly little charges well. And the fish has a much shorter distance from the water to my warehouse, as compared to salmon from Scotland or Norway or Chile. This means that it doesn't have to go into deep freeze. It comes to us at about thirty degrees Fahrenheit—still just below the freezing point, but close enough that the gentle thawing we do before we distribute has minimal effect on the product.

Often, Canadian salmon comes to us as a whole fish. One of the two cutters I have on staff is completely devoted to salmon and salmon alone, slicing and dicing it on-demand to each customer's preferred specifications. Not every distributor has a cutter, because it's expensive to employ one. These are well-paid, highly skilled individuals and get special treatment around the warehouse. I think they're worth every penny, and my clients love it because it saves them labor.

One tell that you're working with quality salmon is its smell. There is zero fishiness. Instead, oddly enough, it has a sweet smell, almost like fresh-cut watermelon. That's another reason I prefer that we do the work ourselves. The entire warehouse smells so good on the days we get a big shipment in.

While whole fish is my preference, market fluctuations mean that you can't always source that, and we have to bring in salmon that's been pre-filleted. It's not ideal, but the demand from my customers is high enough that every now and again you have to take what you can get.

You better know and trust the operations you're buying it from when this is the case. The more processing that happens before it gets to you, the more opportunities there are for something to go wrong. I personally trust the Norwegians when it comes to pre-cut, deep-frozen salmon fillets. I think their product is top-notch without breaking the bank, which is why this is what a lot of high-end country clubs and event catering companies turn to.

The big farming operations in Norway have really streamlined the process, too. They have automatic-filleting machines now, ones that look strangely similar to TSA baggage x-ray machines. Sides of salmon are sent in on a little conveyor belt and scanned by a laser for size and thickness. Then a computer does some lightning-fast geometric calculations, and a split-second later, another, much more powerful laser slices the fish into perfect 8 oz fillets, cleanly and precisely. The beautiful, uniform fillets are individually cryo-vacced and sent to the deep freeze. The whole process is very cool to watch.

You'd never guess that lethal laser beams would have a role in the fishing industry, but they've become the standard, and in my opinion, best way to cut fish on a large scale.

It's the kind of machine that a James Bond villain would have if he decided to give up world domination and turn to aquaculture.

A LOT OF MY customers will ask me for "organic" salmon. It's the kind of buzzword that looks great on a menu, or on the display case at your local fishmonger or grocery store. It implies quality, healthiness, and a concern for the environment.

It's also 100 percent bullshit.

Oh, sure, in theory there's such a thing as organic salmon. You can raise salmon by feeding them only organic food, no antibiotics, everything all-natural, and so on and so on. But in practice, this almost never happens. People don't understand that raising salmon is very different from land-based livestock. You have a lot more control over cattle or chickens or pigs. You can pen them in, keep them isolated, make sure nothing foreign gets into their systems.

This is not the case with raising fish. The most common method for raising fish is to net-off an area of the open ocean. The salmon can't pass through the net, but a hell of a lot of other things can. So you really don't know what they're eating. You can feed them organic food, so you know that at least part of their diet fits the criteria, but they're going to eat whatever they can get their mouths around, so ultimately you don't have a lot of control over it.

Another issue—there's really no agreement on what "organic" means when it comes to fish. There's no governing body of any sort, there's no firmed-up list of rules that's consistent from producer to producer. Organic means basically whatever they say it means. The producer claims to be "certified," but there's no one doing the certifying except themselves.

In the most egregious circumstances, the certification is entirely made up out of whole cloth—by the producers themselves!

Just the other week, a chef from a fancypants golf club in Connecticut told one of my saleswomen that they're only interested in buying certified organic salmon. That's it. That's all they wanted. So I told my saleswoman to back off. Begged her, really. Just stop pitching. Drop the account. Let our competitors have the business. We don't need the hassle, and we definitely don't want to get involved in a pissing contest over a completely arbitrary standard. But this saleswoman, to her credit, wanted the account badly. Not just for the commission, but also for the bragging rights, the ability to say that she'd gotten a foothold in the rarefied air of Blue Blood Connecticut.

So we agreed to the club's requirements, and sourced it as best we could. I personally talked to a producer who I trusted, one who talked a pretty good game about all the measures he'd taken to ensure that his salmon were raised organically. I was still skeptical, but I thought the product was better than most of what was passed off as "organic," so we made the deal.

We delivered a couple of cases to the club at about noon on a Friday. Around 5:00 p.m. that same day, we got a phone call.

Right off the bat, that was a red flag to me. A truly conscientious establishment would have inspected the cases on delivery, immediately. Either the chef themself, or a well-trained receiver is supposed to get eyes on everything that comes into the kitchen right away, so any disputes can be taken care of well before dinner service. And that goes double for a shipment of a new product, or from a new distributor, which we were. But they sat on the cases for hours. The fact that they were only getting around to calling me five hours later meant that this chef had already dropped the ball.

His complaint was that the salmon we'd sent him looked "too wet." He went so far as to send us a picture of our product, next to a picture of our competitor's. And guess what? They looked *exactly the same*. I am pretty sure both pieces of salmon were mine, actually. Plus, neither of them looked wet.

But I heard the guy out. Even when a customer is wrong, he's still a customer, and my impulse is always to make them happy, even if it makes my hair go prematurely grey. After listening for a bit to his complaining, it turns out what had really set him off was that our cases had arrived without a sticker on the outside.

Yes, a sticker. A little sticker that says "organic" to be exact. That's what my competitor's product had. I explained to him that my producer didn't use a sticker. There was, in fact, a little pin on the inside of each case that was my producer's way of showing their organic certification. But the pin wasn't good enough for this chef. He thought I was trying to pull something on him.

Another strike against me, in this guy's mind: I was selling it to him too cheap! In reality, I was giving him an honest markup on what I'd paid for it, but that was still way shy of what he'd been paying my competitor, and it made him suspicious.

So I did some digging. I visited the club to chat with him, and asked to see the packaging for this salmon he'd been paying my competitor a whopping $17.95 a pound for. I recognized the markings immediately. It was regular old farmed Canadian salmon. A fine product, but definitely not organic, and definitely not worth $17.95 a pound.

What was actually happening here was that this rival distributor, when told that this chef only wanted "certified organic" salmon, hatched an idea so stupid, so dishonest, and yet so disarmingly simple that they were able to get away with it for months: they printed their own stickers.

That's right—the "certified organic" stickers that this chef had been so enamored of—his precious guarantee that he was getting the best quality—had been completely fabricated and just slapped on a box. And he hadn't been able to tell the difference.

It reminds me of the line from the immortal Chris Farley in the movie *Tommy Boy*: "If you want me to take a dump in a box and mark it 'guaranteed,' I will. I got spare time." And that's what this chef was getting. An overpriced dump in a box. (But at least it was "certified"!)

Meanwhile, I'm doing things the right way, sourcing exactly what he's asking for, selling it at a cheaper price, and he still thinks that I'm the bad guy. When I told him that he'd been getting snookered, he of course didn't believe me. He was so insulted that I was telling him (in so many words) that he had no fucking idea what he was doing, that he closed the account then and there.

So the moral of the story is, if you see "organic" salmon—or any other kind of seafood, honestly—on the menu, the chances are pretty good that you're being lied to. Whether it was the producer, the distributor, or the restaurant itself, someone in that chain is most likely lying to you. And you're paying the price.

Welcome to the seafood industry in a nutshell.

Chapter 9
LIKE BENNIFER, BUT WITH KNIVES

MAKING A LIVING in the food service industry can be a brutal, thankless lifestyle.

For starters, the hours suck: by definition, you're always working at the times when the rest of the world wants to go out and socialize. Your nights and weekends are not your own. Every holiday is spent slaving over a hot stove instead of with your loved ones.

Making matters worse, the pay is terrible. In most establishments, the staff is just scraping by. Everyone from the bussers all the way up to the head chef is usually barely making ends meet.

It's a stressful job, too, and a physically taxing one. You're on your feet for hours on end with no rest. There's a constant, relentless time crunch, with rushes that can last an entire shift. And to top it all off, you're in a chaotic, dangerous environment with heat and steam and flames, pots and pans clanging, servers and customers and cooks shouting at you, and razor-sharp knives that you know can take off a finger or two if you make a mistake.

Almost every chef I know drinks and smokes way too much. It's their way to cope with all the crushing pressure.

This is not a glamorous way to live.

So why are culinary schools more crowded than ever? Why are people clamoring to pay $38,000 a year to the Culinary Institute of America, when they know that after they graduate, their starting salary as a line cook might not even top $12 an hour? Why are TikTok and YouTube and Instagram filled with people making recipes of all kinds?

Because we are living in the age of the Celebrity Chef.

Television is decidedly better for it. But sometimes I worry that the food world is being destroyed.

WHEN MY FATHER started his business in the seventies, the most famous chef in America was Boyardee. Coming in distant second was Julia Child. Third place was everyone else in a five-hundred-thousand-way tie.

Then, at some point in the mid-nineties, things changed. An obscure cable channel called *The Television Food Network* shortened its name to just *Food Network*. They hired a couple of young, hot-shot NYC chefs named Bobby Flay and Mario Batali, as well as a genial New Orleans wunderkind named Emeril Lagasse.

These were serious cooks, with serious chops, who ran serious restaurants. And then almost overnight, they were seriously famous. Instead of being forced to spend their evenings cooking beef cheek ravioli for thankless yuppies, they instead found themselves trading quips with Jay Leno or throwing out the first pitch at the Mets game.

With the fame came the wealth. Not just the money from the show, but ancillary profits as well: restaurants that were already doing fine were now going gangbusters, fully booked months in advance. Cookbooks topped the bestseller lists. Merchandise soon followed, with cookware, dishware, signature sauces, and spice mixes. The opportunities were seemingly endless: they gave Emeril his own sitcom at one point, for Chrissakes!

(A weird footnote of history was that the show was scheduled to debut on NBC on September 18, 2001—seven days after the planes went into the World Trade Center. The network, thinking that maybe America wasn't ready for the lightly fictionalized antics of a great chef/mediocre actor, wisely pushed the premiere back . . . by a week. Even with the brief delay, America apparently still wasn't ready for it, because it ran for a few weeks to low ratings and critical scorn, and was quietly canceled well before Christmas.)

That early, stunning success of the *Food Network* launched an entire ecosystem. Before long you had *Top Chef* on Bravo, *The Restaurant* on NBC, *The Chew* on ABC, and *Chef's Table* on Netflix. People like Anthony Bourdain, Tom Colicchio, and David Chang became household names, discussed endlessly on the hundreds of food blogs that sprung up, and occasionally even crossing over into the mainstream gossip pages. Glossy food magazines like *Bon Appetit* and *Saveur* that had been around for years took on new relevance.

The gold rush gave cooking for a living a sheen of glitz and glamour. It was suddenly cool to be a chef, and a whole new generation of wannabes —many of whom may have once aspired to simply buckle down at a decent restaurant and cook the best food they could—saw that there was another, more desirable career path.

But people were no longer willing to wait for it. If they didn't have a cookbook deal and a TV show within six months of leaving culinary school, they felt like a failure.

As someone who loves and appreciates food and the people who cook it, this is an alarming turn of events. It's definitely a good thing that more people want to become chefs, but it would be better for them and for all of us if they went into it knowing that they had to pay their dues first.

We need more of the chefs who are truly inspired by art and culture and travel, and draw on this for their ingenuity in the kitchen. We need more people that get behind the stove because they had a lifelong love of food and studied it for years—not because they think it's a good way to get famous.

Instead of knocking on the door of the *Food Network*, I want to see young chefs head to France to apprentice—or *stage*—in the kitchen of a master. Or spend time in a local *boucherie* to learn proper, nose-to-tail butchering techniques; travel Italy for months doing nothing more than learning the perfect technique for handmade pasta; haunt the Toyosu Fish Market in Tokyo to see how the sushi *itamaes* select their glistening cuts of *toro*.

I want my chefs to be inspired by the food, not by the idea of winning a game show.

THAT'S NOT TO say that being a famous chef is inherently bad. There are plenty of instances of chefs who are famous, but remain laser-focused on the most important thing: the food.

I hold up a chef like Eric Ripert as an example of this. He is one of the most famous chefs in the country, thanks to his world-class restaurant Le Bernardin, a veritable temple to seafood in midtown Manhattan, with three Michelin stars. He has appeared multiple times on television over the years, most notably as a guest judge on *Top Chef*. He's the author of several bestselling books. If anyone is a "celebrity chef," it's him.

But his fame seems accidental, not calculated. He's rightfully famous precisely because he's very good at what he does—it doesn't seem like being well-known is his main purpose in life. He's not dollar-chasing either; Le Bernardin still has one location. Aside from a restaurant at the Ritz Carlton in the Cayman Islands that he lent his name to, it's the only place he cooks. He's spending his time making food, not flying all over expanding the concept to branches in Las Vegas and Dubai and Tokyo and Capetown. He seems very content to just continue doing wonderful things in the kitchen, surprising and delighting diners (who, admittedly, shell out a lot of money for the privilege).

Let me pause here to say that I absolutely do not blame those chefs who choose to expand. The odds of a single restaurant being a success, let alone a hit, are so infinitesimally small; and the possibility of financial rewards in this industry are so fleeting; it's completely understandable that when you do strike gold and attain popularity, that you want to keep the gravy train going. And some chefs have navigated this process skillfully. We've already mentioned chef Nobu Matsuhisa, who has expanded his very successful restaurant to almost fifty locations across the globe. But he didn't start expanding until he'd more than established himself as a chef to be reckoned with. You can take issue with the trendiness of his restaurants, or the outrageous pricing, but no one has ever denied the fact that Chef Nobu knows how to serve up truly kick-ass food, first as one of the most renowned sushi makers in LA, and then as a master of Japanese fusion in NYC.

His recipes and concept were apparently good enough to survive and thrive throughout the massive expansion. But Nobu is one of the few exceptions. The truth is that most chefs, even the most talented ones, can't franchise like that, simply because they can't be in more than one place at a time. Truly great chefs are more than just their recipes. They have intangibles that don't necessarily transfer to other locations. There's a certain magic that they impart on the food that may not make it to the plate when they're not physically present in the kitchen. Whether it's their eye for good ingredients, or their palate that can taste and adjust dishes on the fly, or even just the attitude that they impart on their cooks, their restaurants suffer when they're not around.

And those are the *talented* chefs.

The ones with less talent, the ones who skate by because they're good on television? They're going to have trouble even getting off the ground.

Take, for example, a personality from a recent hit show. He was clearly picked by the producers for his looks. More power to him for that, because he's great looking! But it's obvious to anyone who watches the show that he doesn't belong anywhere near a kitchen. His half-assed recipes baffled viewers and drew mockery on social media. But the show was a big enough hit that a few years ago some investors decided that he'd be the perfect face of a new restaurant.

They took over a defunct diner in one of the most stylish neighborhoods in Manhattan, and devised a menu that was filled with on-trend ingredients like avocado, pomegranate, nutritional yeast, and quinoa, and touted each item's friendliness to diets like keto and paleo. (For breakfast, they served a bagel that was "gluten-free, vegan, paleo, grain-free and dairy-free." That sounds like it should be a blatant violation of several New York City penal codes, if not a crime against food itself.)

When the restaurant opened, it was clear that it was less a restaurant and more of a trial run for a potential fast casual franchise. But the reviews were lukewarm, and despite being the subject of several soft-focus profiles in glossy magazines and the *New York Times*, the celebrity chef behind it all was only spotted on the premises intermittently. The place hung around for a few years, but the concept never expanded to other locations. (Understandable, since the market for $16 cauliflower-rice-based lunch bowls is probably limited to three or four zip codes in Manhattan and Los Angeles.) COVID finally put it out of its misery.

I tell this story not to gloat, but as a cautionary tale: the celebrity chef was way out over his skis. Popularity on-screen can only get you so far. If the food isn't good, the restaurant won't be either.

AFTER ALL THIS, you're probably going to be surprised to hear that I'm actually friends with someone who is, much to his chagrin, considered a celebrity chef.

You might remember Hung Huynh as the winner of season three of Bravo's *Top Chef*. He duked it out in Miami against fourteen other chefs, ultimately winning with a tour-de-force meal that included a show-stopping dish: sous vide duck breast with a mushroom and truffle sauce.

Hung's personal story is incredibly inspiring. He was born in Saigon before emigrating with his family at a young age to America. His parents opened a Vietnamese restaurant in Massachusetts, and he started helping in the kitchen at age ten. While he was still in high school, he started cooking at a famous luxury hotel in the Berkshires. He had dreams of going to culinary school, but couldn't afford the tuition. So he bounced around, cooking his way through the country, eventually ending up in Puerto Rico, in the kitchen of the Ritz Carlton hotel. His bosses there felt strongly enough about him that they agreed to fund his degree at the Culinary Institute of America.

After culinary school, Hung worked his way through some prestigious kitchens in New York and Las Vegas. He had only applied to *Top Chef* on a whim, and the notoriety from the show sent the already-promising trajectory of his career into the stratosphere. Suddenly he was more than just a talented cook who was working for other, more established chefs. He was a name unto himself, and restaurateurs came calling.

I met him not long after *Top Chef*. He was in the process of opening a severely cool downtown Manhattan space with nightclub vibes and an enormous, multi-level dining room. Meanwhile, I was pretty early on in my sales career, and his venue was one of my biggest targets. I'd been cold-calling them for weeks, to little effect. I knew that through some sort of sweetheart deal that the owners had set up, the seafood supplier for this particular restaurant was a notoriously bad Philadelphia-based outlet. This distributor was well-known in the industry for pushing cheap products at not-so-cheap prices. The quality was not good, but they were able to undercut the prices of the New York-based distributors by just enough to entice some of the less discerning restaurants into their fold.

All my phone calls were falling on deaf ears, because I couldn't quite match the prices of the Philly guys. But my father had told me that the key to cold-calling was persistence. You never stop, except under very specific circumstances: "When they call the police, that's when you should lay off," he always liked to say. So I kept trying, even though I was still routinely being stonewalled.

You can imagine my surprise then when one day my phone rang and it was the purchasing agent for Hung's restaurant. He said that Hung wanted to meet! I was floored. Not only was this famous chef who I knew could cook his ass off wanting to meet with me, but the request for the meeting came from him! That almost never happens in my line of work. Ninety-nine percent of the time it's the other way around. I'm usually the one doing the hunting. I did a little digging to investigate the reason for my sudden reversal of fortune, and it turns out it wasn't my persistence that had landed me the meeting, in the end.

This time, it was all thanks to some bad crab legs.

In the run up to the opening, Hung had been testing recipes and fussing over ingredients. He was developing a crab leg dish, but couldn't quite get it to the right place. Eventually he came to the realization that the problem wasn't his recipe—it was the product. The Philadelphia suppliers just weren't giving him what he was looking for. Hung visited a chef friend who had his own place nearby, because he remembered an incredible crab dish he'd eaten there a while back. "Where did you get those crab legs?" he asked his friend. "That's exactly what I'm looking for."

"You need to talk to Val's," the chef told him.

After I set the meeting, the big man—Val himself—decided to come with me. I was still pretty new, and he wanted to look over my shoulder a bit as I attempted to close what could be the biggest deal to date in my fledgling career. Plus, the man just liked a good time. A hangout in a cool downtown venue seemed right up his alley.

Hung and my dad hit it off immediately. Val has the natural ability to instantly make friends, and his deep knowledge of all things Asian cuisine (remember, he started his career in Chinatown) just further sealed the deal with Hung. Even though it was technically my deal, I was happy to just sit in the booth and watch a master at work.

After forty-five minutes of laughter-filled conversation, Hung instructed his purchaser to give us the business.

I grew to know Hung very well, and we became genuine friends—a true rarity in this business. We'd go out to dinner together a lot and just blow off steam, talking shit about the industry. And our friendship was mutually beneficial for both our businesses: I'd tip him off when I knew I had something particularly good coming into the shop; he'd return the favor by steering his friends to work with me whenever they opened a new place.

I was constantly impressed by his culinary knowledge, his work ethic, and his open, honest, warm personality. Plus, the dude can just *cook*. He knows food inside and out and is obsessed with perfecting every dish he makes. And he loves to share his obsession with like-minded individuals. When my coauthor Joe and I were visiting with him doing research for this book, he took us into the kitchen at his then-latest restaurant, an Asian fusion concept in Manhattan's formerly-derelict, newly-hip Bowery neighborhood.

He took us into his cooler, and showed us rows and rows of Peking duck hanging from hooks, with fans blowing on them to dry out the skin.

"These will dry out for forty-eight hours," Hung explained, "then we pump them full of air to separate the skin from the meat, which helps it get crispy in the oven."

Later in the dining room, the results of that fastidious process were on full display, with shatteringly crisp skin giving way to the succulent meat underneath. One thing I'll never forget about that meal is that while Joe and I partook of several very good cocktails from the skilled mixologist on staff, Hung only drank glasses of milk. Even though it was supposedly his night off, he wanted to stay sharp to make sure his kitchen was firing on all cylinders.

In the years since, Hung has left New York behind and relocated to Florida. There was some messy business that I don't know the full details of, but he split from the NYC-based restaurateurs he'd been working with. One of his complaints was that his partners—who were mainly focused on opening hip, sceney venues that attracted beautiful people—just didn't take the food component of their business that seriously.

I sympathized deeply with him. He never had aspirations to be a famous chef who slapped his name onto de facto nightclubs; he simply wanted the freedom to cook the best food he possibly could. Though I miss the hell out of him now that he's in the Sunshine State, I can see that he finally found that freedom he's been looking for. He's bouncing between Orlando and Miami, with multiple projects, still cooking the Asian fusion food he's known for, while expanding his repertoire into Greek and Mediterranean cuisine.

I spoke with him recently to get his take on the whole celebrity chef industrial complex. He knows that he owes a good chunk of his success to the fact that he was on TV. While he's skilled enough that he still might have eventually achieved the same culinary heights without becoming a media personality first, the show definitely accelerated his career by several years. He's certainly not ungrateful for it. But he's wary about the effect that sudden fame can have on a young chef who's not necessarily ready for it.

He pointed out that the type of chef that the TV industry is looking to make a star out of is not necessarily the same person that you'd want cooking for you on a regular basis. The TV producers are often looking for "difficult personality types" he says, that will make for more conflict and a more entertaining show. And a lot of the time the producers' first question is "do you look good on camera" instead of "can you cook."

He thinks it's ludicrous that some chefs with limited experience can come directly off a successful TV run and be handed their own restaurant. He had already paid his dues in the industry before he went on TV, so after *Top Chef* he was more than ready to take on his own kitchen. But he sees a lot of newly-minted celebrity chefs taking the shortcut route, and he's worried it might end up reflecting badly on them.

"Why are they opening restaurants? How are they opening restaurants?" he said. "Is it purely because investors approached them like 'Hey, I need a chef. I want to use your name to open my restaurant so I can bring in more of a crowd'? Restaurateurs wouldn't be doing that, though, if there wasn't a demand."

He sees chefs sometimes being put in an impossible situation: "They have to fake it until they make it, because they're not that professional, or not that great at it." But he doesn't blame them for taking the deals that their newfound fame affords them. "Blame that on businessmen. Blame that on the greed of restaurateurs, not chefs."

Hung claims he doesn't keep up with the TV shows that much because he's too busy working. "I honestly don't even have cable," he told me, laughing. But it turns out he's still not completely done with the celebrity chef scene.

In early 2022, just before this book comes out, Bravo will be airing *Top Chef* Season 19, set in Houston, Texas. There will be a panel of previous contestants serving as mentors and judges. And one of them will be a scrappy, outspoken Vietnamese-American chef who loves to drink glasses of milk.

I know I'll be watching.

WHEN I USED to live in Tribeca, the place was just teeming with celebrities. You'd go to get a coffee, or to work out at a yoga studio, and just randomly spot someone like Nikki Hilton or Kirsten Dunst. I was in my favorite bar one time when Kristen Stewart walked in with her absolutely massive security guy. It was completely unnecessary—no one was going to bother her—but that didn't stop her personal bouncer from staring down every person in the room to the point where it was actually uncomfortable.

While the celebrities were the most flashy neighborhood residents (my wife says that Kirsten Dunst is so pretty in person that it actually seems like she's glowing), what Tribeca is really known for are the quiet, nondescript rich people. The types you might share an elevator with, but have no clue that they're the child of a billionaire, or minor European royalty. How could you know? They're just wearing a hoodie on their way out to walk the dog. They don't wear a sign that says "I'm rich" or "I have an important job."

A woman in my apartment building was one of those types. I made friends with her because we belonged to the same gym, and somehow had fallen into the same workout schedule. After a month of seeing her on the treadmill every Saturday morning, I finally struck up a conversation, and it turned out that we were kind of in the same industry!

Make no mistake, she was on the way more glamorous side of things: a talent agent that specialized in celebrity chefs. But we had enough in common that we hit it off immediately. We'd go on double dates—I'd bring my wife, and she her boyfriend—exploring some of the neighborhood restaurants. One year we both attended the Aspen Food and Wine Festival, where she introduced me to one of her clients: Chef Richard Blais, another *Top Chef* winner and a hell of a nice guy.

She seriously knew food, so when she recommended something, I was all ears. One time she started talking about a new place called Toro that was opening up, and I just had to pay attention.

It was a new location, she explained, of a wildly-popular Boston tapas joint. She knew what kind of food I liked, and swore that this was right up my alley: "You will flip over what these guys Jamie and Ken do with food."

She was right. The first time I went, I was just over the moon from the second I walked in. It was a huge warehouse-type space in the Meatpacking District, with a great nineties hip-hop soundtrack and a chef's counter so beautiful—with legs of jamon iberico hanging from the ceilings like chandeliers—that it almost made me cry.

The staff was attentive and just lovely, eager to find you a seat even with no reservation and even more eager to just chat with you. In a city filled with mostly-crappy tapas joints that cater more to the sangria-drinking NYU crowd, this was a godsend. I decided to make it my own.

I frequented so much in those first few months that I got to know every employee. They got to know me in return, and I was gratified when they started treating my arrivals with fanfare, announcing to the downstairs kitchen "He's back!" whenever I stepped into the dining room.

I was voracious for the food. I'd beg my wife to go two, three, four times a week. When she begged off, saying she needed a break, I'd go by myself but still order the same amount of dishes as if she was there with me. The waitstaff definitely thought I was insane, but they seemed to love me all the more for it.

My legend grew, and eventually the head honchos caught wind of this food-obsessed maniac who was ordering twenty to twenty-five dishes by himself and having no problem finishing them all, washing everything down with copious amounts of scotch. So one night the chefs and co-owners Jamie Bissonette and Ken Oringer came to my table and introduced themselves. They were very sweet, and thanked me for my patronage, which they'd heard was so over the top that they felt compelled to meet me.

I explained to them how much I loved their food, and that there are few restaurants I care to frequent because (let's face it) I'm kind of a pain in the ass, and hard to please. After that ice-breaking, anytime I was at the restaurant on the same nights as Jamie, he would come out of the kitchen to chat. He'd give me off-menu tastes, and tell me about the new recipes he was trying out, sometimes sending dishes my way and asking my opinion before deciding to officially put them on the menu. When his book came out, he signed a copy for me, and I proudly display it in my library to this day.

This went on for months, as a purely friendly relationship. It wasn't business-related at all. In fact, it was a quite a while before he even realized what I did for a living. Once he figured that out, of course we had a whole new subject to talk about, and he'd always pick my brain about the market for shrimp or king crab.

And above all, he especially loved to talk about octopus.

This was one item that I happened to have a particularly great handle on. I loved the ingredient, and from the beginning of my time with the company, I pushed for us to expand our footprint in the space. Today, we are one of the largest distributors of Spanish octopus in the country.

Eventually, it was inevitable that we'd start to do business together. I made sure that Toro had the best products at a fraction of what they'd be paying from a competitor. I took special care of this account, because I loved the restaurant, and I cherished Jamie and Ken and all their talented staff. When you meet people that are that passionate about the same things you are, you just want to be a part of it. I was barely breaking even on the account, but I didn't care; I didn't feel the need to make a killing off of them. This was a personal mission for me. I felt like I was doing God's work helping talented chefs deliver consistent, quality products to their patrons—and, selfishly, to me.

Even after I moved out of the city and to a small town in Connecticut, and wasn't able to frequent Toro as much, I stayed in constant contact with Jamie. We both have bulldogs and share pictures and stories of their every idiotic, adorable moment. I like to send him pictures of the food I make, the pizzas and steaks I cook in my outdoor kitchen. I know that he, as a James Beard Award–winning chef, probably isn't that impressed by my little backyard cooking experiments, but he always at least pretends to be, so I appreciate it.

When I do ask him for help with my cooking, he's always quick with advice. And he's even quicker to extend generosity. Like when the pandemic hit, I asked him if he could share a paella recipe with me to promote our newly-formed direct to consumer business. With his guidance, we created a cook-at-home paella kit, and promoted it as Jamie's recipe. There he was, one of the most talented chefs in the country, who would have no trouble getting money for sharing his recipe, but he just gave it to me for free because he wanted to help. To this day I am thankful for his kindness.

He's also acted as a sounding board for this book. For example, he gave me a different perspective on the topic of celebrity chefs.

(Now, I'd consider Jamie to be a celebrity chef, even if he doesn't fit the definition of the term as we've been using it here. He's done a little bit of TV, including winning an episode of the *Food Network* game show *Chopped*. But his fame doesn't come from his media appearances. He earned it the old-fashioned way, by cooking incredible food that people want to eat.)

Nevertheless, as Jamie sees it, the whole topic of celebrity chefs lends itself to a net positive: "Celebrity chefs have been good for the industry," he told me, "because prior to the chef being celebrated, they weren't even allowed inside the dining room."

The more I thought about it, the more I realized he was right. There are a lot of negative aspects of the celebrity chef, but ultimately it raises the profile of all the men and women who make our food, and makes their profession something that's more sought after, and more exciting than ever before. That's gotta be a good thing for everyone in the business, myself included.

Toro is closed now, a victim of COVID, but Jamie is still doing fine. His latest venture with Ken, Little Donkey, is about the coolest world cuisine restaurant I've ever seen. Nestled in Cambridge, near Harvard University, it has an atmosphere that most restaurateurs would kill for: an airy room with exposed brick and high ceilings. But the ambiance is come by honestly—there's nothing manufactured or calculated about it. The food at Little Donkey is always evolving, and of course always delicious. I was lucky enough to attend their friends and family soft opening, and I knew right away that if I didn't live several hours away it was the kind of place that I'd practically move into, I'd be there so many nights a week for dinner.

The funny thing is that when you find someone who cooks food that entices you, that draws you in—food that grabs tight onto your taste buds and won't let go—it ultimately doesn't matter how many times they've been on TV. Because from that point on, they're always going to be a celebrity to you.

Chapter 10
RESTAURANTNOMICS

IF I RAN my business as badly as most restaurants run theirs, I'd have to close my doors within a month.

I know it's hard for restaurants in the COVID world, and everyone is struggling to get by, but if some of these places spent even a fraction of as much time and energy attempting to get a handle on their finances as they do trying to skip out on bills, they'd be on much more solid ground.

The restaurant industry runs on credit. Specifically, credit extended to them by me and my fellow distributors. This is unsecured credit, mind you. I'm not a bank, even though I'm often treated as one.

Ideally, suppliers would always get paid on delivery. That's how it works in most of the rest of the world. You walk into a store, you buy a candy bar, you give the guy a dollar, and you walk out. Transaction over. Everyone is happy.

But in the food world, I'm expected to deliver thousands, tens of thousands, or sometimes even hundreds of thousands of dollars worth of product to a restaurant every week, on time with no delay. But they don't have to pay me back right away. They have thirty days to do so. Most of the time they do. A lot of the time they don't.

One of my customers is a high-end Greek restaurant. This isn't your corner gyro joint. This is a place with incredible seafood dishes that costs $100 to $200 a head once you factor in appetizers and drinks.

They are very well-regarded by critics and diners, and I sort of get the impression that all this clout is what makes them feel like they don't have to pay us in a timely manner.

I actually cut them off one time. They were too far behind on bills, and I told them we didn't need their business anymore. It only took them a week to come crawling back to us, begging for us to sell to them again. They clearly realized that we have the best product in town, and all the adulation from critics and customers wasn't going to help them if they weren't putting top-notch food on the plates.

So after they'd coughed up a bit of money, we started selling to them again. Except this time, I jacked up my prices. I wasn't doing this to be vindictive. This was my insurance policy. I had to protect my own business, and if they welched again I wanted a nice cushion to soften the blow. I also told them that their thirty-day payment window was now fourteen days. They agreed, and things were good again for a while.

Flash forward a few months later, my dad had a hankering for Greek food and invited me to come with him. He asked the salesman in charge of the account to get him a reservation. I told him this was a bad idea. Begged and screamed for him to reconsider. If he wanted to eat there, fine, but I wanted our visit to be a little more under the radar. *Let's just get the reservation the normal way. Don't give them a heads up that we're coming.* Because I knew what was going to happen if we went in there as suppliers instead of civilians.

I should explain that one of my father's most winning personality traits is that he's Mr. Affable. He wants to be everyone's friend. He can be a hard-nosed business guy when he wants to be, but he'd much rather be a pal. Personally, I don't want to be pals with most of my customers, especially ones with a history of playing fast and loose with paying me. Your "pals" have a tendency to assume that your friendship gives them some extra leeway when it comes to giving you money on time.

But the ball was already rolling. The salesman got us the reservation, and when we showed up for our dinner, the red carpet was rolled out. Best table in the house, lots of comped drinks and small plates, plenty of schmoozing from the manager and the chef and the owner himself. It was a lovely dining experience. The food was delicious. I had a great time with my old man.

And yet I knew as we paid our bill and left the restaurant that the other shoe was inevitably going to drop.

Sure enough, lo and behold the next week we get the phone call: "We can't pay you this week. But we still need our delivery."

Thanks a lot, *pal.*

YOU MIGHT BE thinking that this sounds like extraneous griping. Just me complaining about problems that are very specific to me and my business, but aren't the concern of the average person who just wants to go out for a nice meal. But I promise you that this type of behavior has a ripple effect that can lead to things going very wrong for the average American diner.

Deadbeat restaurateurs in the long run will end up paying a lot more for their ingredients than the ones who pay up on time. The cost of their negligence is something that I—and everyone else who supplies them—will price into every delivery order. And that premium will eventually be passed onto you, the person eating there, whether that's in the form of higher prices on the menu or lower-quality food on the plate.

In New York City, the Health Department inspects restaurants and gives them letter grades for cleanliness that they're required to display prominently in their front windows. A lot of people will check for the "A" in the window, and eat somewhere else if they see a "B" or a "C." But maybe there should be an agency that looks at a restaurant's credit and assigns them a grade for that instead. That would be a much more helpful measure of whether or not a restaurant is going to give you food poisoning, in my opinion.

The aforementioned Greek restaurant is actually not even the worst-case scenario. They at least put in the bare amount of effort at maintaining a relationship with us, because they still want our product. A lot of restaurants faced with a growing bill will simply walk away.

Restaurants are constantly threatening to take their business elsewhere. Sometimes it's to prove a point. Sometimes it's simply a negotiating tactic to try and obtain cheaper prices. Either way, they're incredibly cold-blooded about it. They almost never call you and say, "Hey, can we work something out?" There's rarely a negotiation. All the rapport and the relationship-building that my salesmen and I put effort into go completely out the window.

They are simply your customer one day . . . and the next day, not.

Some people might say this is a shrewd business tactic, or "they're just being ruthless," but it's neither of those things. It's counterproductive and frankly lazy. Instead of working through their problems, they go for the quick and easy solution: leave me in the lurch and find someone else who will put up with their bullshit.

Competition amongst distributors is fierce enough that at first a restaurant won't have to look too far for a willing patsy. I see many of my competitors extending credit way beyond what's prudent as a means to win business. The industry standard for someone in good standing is thirty days until payment. If you want to keep a restaurant on a tighter leash, you might knock them down to fourteen or seven days. But when attempting to win over new accounts, I've seen some distributors make crazy offers like "you can pay me in sixty days." Whenever I see standards that relaxed, I know a restaurant is about to get some shit product jammed down their throat.

When we lose an account, it's certainly a downer. That's money lost for the company, and commission lost for a salesman. But I always tell them don't let it ruin your day. Because more often than not, the accounts come back. When a company has better products, service, and is easier to work with like we are, the customer always comes back! (Not to mention, we often do have the lowest prices. We are large enough that even with selling mostly high-end ingredients, our economy of scale means that we can secure large amounts of product at an advantageous price.)

"Just wait, they'll be back" isn't much of a consolation to a salesman who loses a major account and has trouble seeing anything beyond the money flying out of his own pocket. But this can often lead to even bigger paydays for them down the line. When a customer comes crawling back, hat-in-hand, two or three months later, that's when I start seeing dollar signs. When a salesman comes to me and starts the conversation with, "You'll never believe it . . . " that's when I know I'm about to get a big payday.

The wayward customers will come up with all kinds of mealy-mouthed justifications for why they're suddenly returning, but I'm already counting my cash. They might be saying, "We'd like to touch base and get pricing on some items that we used to buy from you," but all I'm hearing is "CHA-CHING."

Because when these guys come back, I know that's my license to print money. Returning to the table is just their way of telling me that they know we're the best, and they made a huge mistake by leaving in the first place. They don't put it in those words, of course. But I can read between the lines.

They might think that they're doing me a favor wanting to do business again, but they don't realize that they're now in what I call the "penalty box." They were getting fair market pricing before, but now they're on my shit list, so they're going to get hammered.

Once again—this is not me being vindictive! Well . . . maybe a little. But mostly this is because I now know that I can't trust this owner anymore. They've already shown that they're willing to walk away. They were happy to stiff me on the bill, and take a two-by-four to our hard-built business relationship. So I'm not going to stick my neck out for them anymore. If they want to act like an angry third grader, I'll treat them accordingly, putting them in the business world equivalent of "timeout" and doing what it takes to protect myself and my people going forward.

So now they're going to pay a premium. They're not getting sweet-heart deals anymore. And they're going to have a smaller window to pay me and a lot less leeway in general.

In a way, a customer leaving and then coming back is the great-est gift they can give me. They found out the hard way that the grass is decidedly not greener out there, and now I know that I must have something that no one else in town can give them. They played their stupid little game, and now it's my turn to jam them for as much money as humanly possible.

Case in point: In summer 2021, one of my biggest customers—a multi-state restaurant and nightclub group—tried to take their business elsewhere. We were selling to this company's locations in NYC, Miami, LA, Vegas, all over. Then overnight, poof! It was all gone. Completely cut off.

My first order of action was to do . . . nothing. I know the game, and whoever blinks first is almost always the loser.

Now, if this had been termination for cause—if we had done something wrong, or there had been a problem, I would have been a veritable whirlwind trying to fix it. Phone calls, in-person visits, flying across the country, you name it. If the problem is on my end, I'm going to go above and beyond trying to repair the relationship.

But that wasn't this. This was more of the usual power games. They didn't want to pay, or they wanted lower prices, or they had some unspecified grievance. So I did nothing. They didn't give me the courtesy of explaining why the orders had stopped, and I wasn't going to embarrass myself begging for them to start buying again.

So I waited it out.

Cut to six weeks later. I was coincidentally taking my first real day off in more than a year. I'd been on-duty pretty much non-stop since the pandemic started, and it was only in June 2021 that I felt things had settled enough that I could finally take some well-deserved R and R.

Of course that's when the phone call came. I took it, because I knew what was coming: a big fat apology.

I listened to their sob story, and I said all the right things in response. "I totally understand, it's just business, this happens all the time, happy to work with you again" and so on. And that wasn't a lie. I was plenty happy to work with them again. But it was going to be on my terms.

"So here's the deal: if you want to work with us again, I'm going to need a deposit of $10k. And your payment window is no longer thirty days. Now it's seven. Also, since you left, we've increased prices."

You may think this sounds onerous, or punitive, but they obliged, happy to get access again to the product that they'd clearly had trouble sourcing without my help. They sent us the required deposit, and are currently paying promptly every week. Meanwhile, I managed to increase my margin dramatically.

They were the assholes in this situation, and it only ended up working out in my favor.

IF YOU CAN believe this, restaurants bounce checks all the time. When a restaurant bounces a check, they are telling you a few things. One is they are poor money managers and even worse business people. The simple fact that you're supposed to be a solvent, responsible enterprise, and you're out there writing bum checks is mind-boggling to me. But it happens quite a bit, unfortunately.

I take something like that seriously. A restaurant that's delinquent on its bills is one thing. That's not great, but it's kind of par for the course in this industry. But a restaurant that's actively passing bad paper around town? That's not only a waste of my time; it's a threat to my business. If your books are so bad that you can't cover a check you write, that's a sign to me that you don't have a handle on your shit, and that you could go down at any time, leaving me holding the bag.

So I respond appropriately. I not only charge restaurants a bloated fee for that bounce, but I also start jacking up their prices 20 to 30 percent. I'm not doing this to be evil. I'm simply trying to preemptively protect myself from what I see as a ticking time bomb. I'm extracting as much money from you as I can before you inevitably explode.

When you bounce a check, you're telling me that you don't even care about your own business and employees, so I know there's no way you care about mine.

Dig into the books of any restaurant that has cash flow problems like that, and you'll inevitably find an owner who is paying himself first. As a business owner myself, I know that I'm the last one to get paid. My employees, my suppliers, and the dozens of other interested parties that I owe money to are all in line ahead of me before I see a dime. I accept that. Some owners don't. They treat their restaurants like a piggy bank, emptying the till at the end of the night into their own pocket like a junkie.

When a restaurant that's mismanaged like that eventually explodes, it can have the potential for tremendous collateral damage. Suppliers, vendors, and employees get left holding the bag while the owner uses tricky financial maneuvering to get himself off the hook, and in some cases, start over with a clean slate.

I've seen it hundreds of times—a failing restaurant will "reorganize" or simply change their name. That's essentially a form of declaring bankruptcy. They're allowed to keep operating and making money, but they are no longer responsible for past bills. It's a pretty shrewd move, honestly, from their point of view. It's funny how all these guys seem dumb with money until their back is up against the wall, then they suddenly become tricky and leave people like me in the lurch.

When a restaurant goes under and does not settle their bills, there's a domino effect that ripples throughout the entire small ecosystem of businesses that work with them. I'm in a somewhat privileged position, in that I'm one of the larger companies and can absorb some losses. But there are plenty of smaller mom and pop vendors who are devastated when they get stiffed like that. They might even lose their own businesses in the process.

Have you ever seen a restaurant in your town undergo a "renovation" or suddenly change their name, but serve the same food under the same owner? Behind that decision is a trail of tears of vendors who did not get paid.

To MITIGATE THE risk of restaurants going out of business (or simply deciding to not pay their bill), we use a service that insures some of our receivables. For this peace of mind I pay about $100k a year. It's not a huge payment in the scheme of things, but it's just one more thing to add to the list of line items, the cost of which gets inevitably passed on to my customers, and eventually to *their* customers—a.k.a. you, the average diner.

You probably know at this point in the book that I'm nothing if not transparent, so I'm going to be radically honest about my business here. Let's talk for a bit about my overhead.

In addition to my aforementioned $100k a year insurance, here's a rough look at my monthly outlays:

Payroll—$240k a month

Payroll taxes—$100k a month

Medical insurance—$20k a month

Gas for my truck fleet—$20k a month

401k contributions—$25k a month

Auto insurance for my trucks—$10k a month

Electricity and heating for the office and warehouse—$6k a month

Parking tickets—$5k a month (and this is actually low for a New York City–based distributor)

Property taxes—$4k a month

Phone & Internet—$1k a month

That's about $430,000 a month, every month—NOT INCLUDING THE COST OF PRODUCT. Just to keep my lights on, even if I don't I sell a single shrimp or salmon fillet, it costs me about $5 million a year. And that's not even counting the dozens of other unpredictable costs that crop up on a regular basis—flat tires, broken freezers, business dinners, the company Christmas party—the list goes on, endlessly.

I'm not sharing this with you to complain about it. I know better than anyone that you gotta spend money to make money. But I want you to understand why I seem so profit-driven sometimes. I've got thirty-five people who depend on me for their living. I can't just tell them, "Oh, it was a bad month. Can we have two more weeks to make payroll?" Or I can't just say, "I don't feel like paying on time for my Internet service," and tell Optimum to fuck off. As much as I'd like to. (I'm still mad at them from early on in the pandemic when my phones stopped working inexplicably, and weren't fixed for almost a month. That's just what you need when you're trying to bail out a business that had the rug completely pulled out from under it.)

I have obligations, so I have to have an eye on my profits at all times. I have to seek out the big paydays, because every time my truck makes a stop, it costs me somewhere between $50 and $70. I have to make at least that much profit on each sale simply to break even.

The bad news is these obligations actually prevent me from working with a lot of people I'd otherwise love to be in business with. Some smaller restaurants are simply not profitable enough for me to service.

It's a shame, because I know some of these places are run by fastidious chefs who truly care about the quality of the product, but they're not operating at a volume that's going to make it worth my while.

(One time I was looking to acquire another smaller seafood company, and in the process I got a peek at their books. They specialized in servicing the highest of the high-end eateries, with some of the best-sourced, most rare, sought-after and expensive ingredients, yet their margins were crap. I asked the owner why they weren't making any money servicing restaurants with honest-to-God Michelin stars.

"Allen," he said, "we have to go to these places every single day, and the orders can fit into a paper bag." Instead of the more cost-effective method of delivering large orders once or twice a week, he was doing minuscule orders all week long. No wonder he wasn't making any money! That just reinforced for me why I, as a distributor, was not interested in that type of business. We like dropping pallets not paper bags. I ended up passing on acquiring that company.)

So we try to do business with big users that can order multiple items from us at a time. The sweet spot for us is an account that nets me about $200 to $500 every time one of my trucks stops there. We're talking something in the range of five hundred to a thousand pounds of product a week for us to make any real money. I know there are some restaurants out there that only seat twenty people at a time doing some exciting things; I know there are some critically-acclaimed chefs doing tasting menus that only need small quantities of one or two very specific items from me. It would be a feather in my cap to work with these people, for the bragging rights more than anything. But a lot of the time I have to very reluctantly pass on that kind of business.

It's New York City's fault, honestly.

NYC is almost impossible to do business in at this point. If you are a food distributor—doing your part to feed the city and to stimulate the economy—you're getting fucked over in a million different ways.

The biggest point of conflict is with my drivers. Being a delivery driver in Manhattan is one of the toughest jobs I can think of. Traffic is ridiculous. Streets are constantly closing for random events. Parking rules are all over the map and change on a daily basis. So my drivers are often—through no fault of their own—running behind, and even when they do get to their delivery location, they're forced to double park to unload. That's when they run into trouble with the NYPD.

I told you about the $5k a month in parking tickets that my guys rack up. That's thanks to ticket-happy cops who find any excuse they can to slap my drivers with infractions. The police will deny it, but they have a major hard-on for delivery drivers. I've been told on good authority that the orders came from the top to target those who drive for a living, while ignoring the many infractions of private motorists. You can spot this at any corner of the city, a traffic cop taking twenty minutes to berate a delivery driver while directly behind him private cars run red lights and pull U-turns with impunity. The theory is that cops do this because the professional drivers won't fight the tickets. Their companies eat the cost, chalking it up to just the expense of doing business. (It is definitely a cost of doing business, but that still doesn't mean I have to like it. We've actually hired a service that in exchange for a monthly fee will negotiate down the cost of our tickets.)

When COVID first hit, we noticed our drivers were getting slapped with infractions like crazy. I don't know if it was because there were just fewer cars on the road so my trucks stood out even more than usual, or if it was just a case of the cops being more anxious and bored than usual. But either way, we were getting slammed like never before.

Keep in mind that at that point, with most restaurants in the city closed or at least severely curtailed, we didn't even know if we'd be able to stay in business. The few deliveries that we did have were a blessing. So when one of my drivers came back to the shop after a short run of two deliveries and told me that in the process he'd gotten three tickets, I hit the roof. Apparently, in the course of lecturing him, a maskless cop had even forced his hand right into the cab of the truck and turned the hazard blinkers off, just to prove a point or something. The hostility toward people just trying to earn a living was out of control.

Another way the city of New York works against you is the Business Integrity Commission. Certain industries—carting, wholesale marketers and distributors, waste haulers—are required to register with this government agency every other year and pay outrageous dues. The

Commission was started, supposedly, to keep organized crime out of the waste management industry. But in the process, they've come up with a set of regulations so onerous that it's almost like they're the Mafia themselves! Every time I talk to a Commission rep I feel compelled to ask why they even exist as an organization. They have the nerve to tell me it's for *my* protection.

Does that sound familiar to you? Is there another entity you can think of that extorts money from legitimate businesses and claims to provide "protection"?

Their tactics are incredibly heavy-handed. When they found out that my dad was retiring and I was taking over, they swarmed my warehouse with twenty armed officers wearing bulletproof vests. They forced paperwork on me, letting me know that I was obligated to complete it and join the Commission. The paper was fifty pages long, and seemed designed to suss out whether or not I was a crook, asking random questions like what does my spouse do for a living, and what kind of gifts did I get for my wedding. (I was very tempted to fuck with them and lie that I had gotten nothing but gold pinky rings, track suits, and sawed-off shotguns, but I didn't think they'd find that particularly amusing.)

The agency was created back in the Giuliani administration. Since he had made his bones as a US attorney fighting organized crime, it only seemed natural that he'd create an entity to continue the fight as a mayor. But in the intervening years, the BIC has swollen to the point where it's threatening to gobble up multiple businesses and industries.

It's a shakedown, plain and simple, and they're not even doing that good a job of catching the bad guys. Right now, for example, one of my competitors is busy carrying out a scam of epic proportions. He "laid off" all his employees, and currently has them off the books working for cash. If the Commission can't even catch that kind of *barely-organized* crime, how can they ever hope to take on the Mafia?

If they were truly interested in preserving the integrity of the industry, they'd be doing something like making sure invoices actually matched products being sold, or doing spot-checks of crates to determine if the listed weight matches the actual weight. Those are the kinds of tiny cheats that compromise the integrity of this industry, but there's zero oversight. (To be fair, I don't actually want them to do this, because that would be disruptive and onerous as well. But it would still be better than what they're currently doing.)

Refrigeration is another area that should be regulated, but is completely ignored by the BIC. Ideally, meat, produce, and especially seafood should be delivered in trucks that are temperature-controlled. Especially in the summer, the quality of products can be severely compromised after just a few minutes in a hot vehicle. I spend a ton of time and money maintaining my trucks. Each one is well-insulated and fitted with a state-of-the-art refrigeration system. But there are plenty of operations out there delivering in rickety cargo vans, or—even worse—open-bed pickup trucks.

For evidence of this, just go to any Restaurant Depot (that's a chain of wholesalers with massive, warehouse-like retail locations—basically, a Sam's Club for restaurants) and check out the parking lot. Look at the vehicles in the lot. You'll see maybe 5 percent of them, tops, with refrigeration. I understand that it's expensive to install the climate-control—probably somewhere in the realm of $10k per truck—but it's so necessary that I can't believe the Commission won't step in. Why are they hassling me, who does everything by the book, when there are plenty of other guys loading boxes of shrimp onto scorching-hot metal truck beds, only to melt in the hot sun and spoil before they make their way to someone's plate?

THERE'S A WELL-KNOWN (trust me, you've heard of it) restaurant in downtown New York that has branches in Las Vegas and Miami and are eying other locations, so they clearly aspire to be a national or even global brand. They were using this incredibly sought-after scampi from New Zealand. (A quick digression—in America, "scampi" is the name of a dish, namely shrimp prepared in a white wine and garlic sauce. But authentic scampi—also known as langoustine, Dublin Bay prawn, or Norway lobster—is actually a separate species. They are about the size of shrimp, but have an anatomy closer to a lobster. They are incredibly delicate and delicious, and notoriously difficult to procure and ship. Pound-for-pound they are more expensive than lobster, and it's very likely that you've never eaten one, even if you think you have.) Anyway, these New Zealand scampi are not easy to come by. You really need to have a good relationship with a supplier, a good business reputation, and of course plenty of money to pay for this specific product up front before you can get it into the States. There are many imposters out there that do not process and package them correctly. They are extremely perishable, and if they're not cared for properly at every step of the shipping process they begin to spoil from the inside-out. Their heads turn black, the flesh begins to shrink, and they end up completely inedible.

For these reasons, not a lot of people seek them out, but this customer was very insistent on this particular product, and we wanted to please them, so we secured as much of it as we could. For our trouble, we charged them north of $22 a pound, with a new shipment coming every week.

The customer was happy and was particularly good at paying us on time, usually on a COD basis. Occasionally they'd beg off paying and ask us to deliver on credit, paying us a week later. They still always paid, so it wasn't anything to get alarmed at yet, but their product was special-ordered, and it would be potentially difficult to find another buyer if they fell through as a customer. So I started paying special attention to their account.

Soon enough, their one-week delays turned into two. Then three. And then they were four weeks behind. Clearly they were having cash flow issues. So I suggested to the owner that we take a pause on the langoustines while they got their finances in order.

"Oh no, we must have the New Zealand scampi! Our customers expect it. In fact, we need more this Friday."

I respected the fact that they were insistent on using the best. A lot of restaurants in their position would have quietly swapped out the ingredient for something a lot cheaper, betting that their diners wouldn't even notice the difference. And that would have been a safe bet! But whether it was out of a true commitment to quality, or simply a misplaced sense of pride, they wanted to keep going with one of the most rare and expensive delicacies the sea had to offer, delinquent bills be damned.

I was happy to continue to provide it to them, but I sure as shit wasn't going to be left holding the bag!

So I told them they could have the new product in time for their weekend dinner service, but it was going to cost them. The price was going up, they were going to have to pay me up front, and they also owed me an 18 percent finance charge on their outstanding debts. They grumbled about it, but you know what—they paid me. That's how the New Zealand scampi that should have cost them $22 a pound ended up costing them more than $50.

And if you think they ate that cost, well, I have a beautiful bridge that spans the East River to sell you. They passed that on to their customers, of course!

Yet another illustration as to why you should always run in the other direction when you see "Market Price" on the menu. You're not necessarily paying the cost of the food. You could be secretly paying the cost of the restaurant's mismanagement of its own money!

A few years back I hired a friend of mine who was a true finance whiz. He had a heap of Ivy League degrees, including a Wharton MBA. His resume read as a who's-who of the private equity world. But he was looking to expand into other fields, and I felt like we could use his expertise, so I brought him in to see if there was any way he could streamline our financials.

Right off the bat, he was stunned at the way we did things in the restaurant world. Keep in mind, this was a guy who was well-versed in complex business arrangements, several of which he'd even set up himself! But the fundamentals of this very messy industry were still shocking to him.

He couldn't fathom the amount of credit we extended to our customers, or why they'd continue to get deliveries when their debts were so outstanding. Another common practice that he couldn't wrap his head around was when restaurants would sometimes return product to us a few days after delivery, claiming some problem or other with the quality. We'd crack open the returned case and find nothing wrong with it, but still had to eat the loss.

"Allen, I'm pretty sure this is a scam," he told me one Monday while we were inspecting the latest return. "It seems to me that these guys took a shipment on Friday, weren't able to sell any of it over the weekend, and just made something up as an excuse to send it back."

"That's exactly what happened," I told him. "That happens all the time."

"So why do you take it back?"

I shrugged. "It's just what restaurants do. They do it with all their distributors. They've always done it that way."

I agreed with his outsider's perspective that it was, on its face, insane to have a policy like that. It was very hard for this guy coming from a different, more buttoned-up corner of the business world to look at the very turbulent relationship between distributors and white tablecloth dining establishments, and see anything but chaos and inefficiency. But it's a give and take situation. I have to sometimes turn a blind eye to my customers' shady or even borderline-abusive behavior with the idea that I'll make it up down the line. They might ding me a couple times a year with returned product, or a delinquent payment, but I'm thinking long-term. If I can maintain the relationship, I'm seeing profits for years to come.

It's sort of the same stance you see from retailers like Costco. They have a famously generous return policy. They'll take anything back, no matter the condition, even years after the purchase. I read once about a woman who showed up at a Costco in January with a Christmas tree she'd purchased six weeks earlier. It was brown and dry, needles falling off. The clerk asked her why she was returning it. She said "because it's dead."

They gave her a full refund.

What Costco and I both understand is that it's a long game. Even with a short-term loss, keeping the customers on the hook will pay off in the end.

Chapter 11
THE TWO DREADED LETTERS

I'VE TOLD YOU already about my disdain for seeing "Market Price" on a menu. Nine times out of ten, it has no actual basis in how much the restaurant paid for the ingredient; it's just a way for them to hide the ball on a big-ticket, high-margin item that they want to trick you into ordering.

But that's not to say that the cost of seafood doesn't fluctuate. It's an item that's sourced from all over the world, from thousands of disparate suppliers each dealing with their own issues. The price can fluctuate based on a variety of factors—seasonality, weather, the price of boat fuel, shipping capacity, political unrest—not to mention, good old-fashioned supply and demand: if a catch is especially large or small, or if an ingredient suddenly becomes very popular or unpopular.

The fact that most seafood freezes so well helps to smooth out a lot of the wild price swings. With careful planning, intuition, and occasionally educated guesswork, I can stock up on an item when my suppliers' price is low, and avoid buying when it's high. I have a skilled team of purchasers who all have twenty to forty years experience, reading the market and strategically buying millions of dollars of product months in advance. But sometimes, especially with the most expensive, most sought-after ingredients that Val's Ocean Pacific specializes in—or, more recently, with all the COVID disruptions—nothing can be done. On these rare occasions, I'll end up having to buy near the top of the market, and am forced to pass that cost along to my customers. After all, I can't afford to sell at a loss. I can't even really afford to sell at "break even." Remember, I've got bills to pay!

I've talked a lot about restaurants that backslide on quality—namely when they order only the best stuff as they're still establishing a name, but switch over to cheaper product once they've achieved a certain level of popularity. Not every restaurant operates this way, though. There are plenty of chefs and owners, I've found, that have enough integrity and/or ego that once they commit to bringing a certain level of quality to their dining room, they're very reluctant to cut corners in the name of saving money.

For restaurants that aren't chasing trendy, fickle clientele—restaurants that are in it for the long haul—maintaining a certain level of quality is essential. These established restaurants depend on repeat business. Their regular customers are, by definition, loyal. But their loyalty only goes so far. And they're more knowledgeable than the average customer that walks in off the street, so if items that they've ordered time and again suddenly change, they're a lot more likely to notice it. Keeping these customers on the hook, so to speak, is an essential part of a restaurant's business model. In a way, they are operating a subscription-based service, just as much as Amazon Prime or Netflix is.

But not every restaurant has that much foresight. They're not looking ahead years down the line. They're just looking to fill their walk-in for the next week's dinner service. Market Price acts as a pressure release valve for their lack of planning. It allows them to boost their margins in a sneaky way to make up not necessarily for the cost of the ingredients, but for other shortfalls in their books.

FRESH TUNA IS an example of one of those products that's prone to wild fluctuations in price, usually on a monthly basis. Tuna are a migratory species, so the fishermen chasing them around don't always have an easy time catching them, and the cost reflects that. It's always been this way. Restaurants could plan for this, and hedge their bets accordingly.

But at this point in the book it probably won't surprise you when I tell you: they absolutely do not do this.

As soon as the price of tuna starts creeping up, even as much as $1 extra per pound, I've got dozens of angry chefs, owners, and receivers screaming at me on the phone about how "this is an outrage" and "we're going to take our business elsewhere."

It falls to me or one of my salespeople to talk them down off the ledge.

My first strategy in these situations is always to convince them to "stay in the pocket." That is, don't change their purchasing. *The bump in price,* I tell them, *is just temporary. A week, maybe two, tops. If they downgrade their ingredients now, they'll regret it later. It's going to hurt their business in the long run. They're a special breed of restaurant. Their diners expect the best, and are discerning enough to know when they're not getting it anymore,* and so on and so on.

This argument works on a decent percentage of people.

But not everyone, of course. Some people are so price-sensitive that no amount of smooth-talking is going to keep them in the fold. So my next step is to offer them options.

The best quality fresh tuna is known as #1, which goes generally for $16 to $18 a pound. The next tier of fresh is 2+ at about $14 to $15 a pound. After that, if you want to go even lower in price, you have frozen, which is where you start seeing big savings: top-quality frozen loin goes for $7 to $8 a pound, and pre-cut into steaks it's $5 to $6. (The pre-cut is cheaper because it's an inferior product to whole loin. In my opinion, tuna should not be cut down until as close to serving as possible. It should remain as a loin and cut to order. Cutting it just exposes more surface area to air, and causes the meat to deteriorate faster.)

There is nothing inherently wrong with frozen tuna, especially the stuff I get, that's well-processed and cared for at every step of the distribution chain. And the beauty of frozen is that the price never budges. It's a very stable cost year round, so that layer of predictability is built in. It's a very tempting product, especially when you factor in that not a lot of diners—even the aforementioned most discerning ones—will be able to tell the difference.

So this presents a real quandary to the restaurant. Sure, they could save a ton of money using that frozen eight-ounce tuna steak that I sold them for $5.50 a pound. And chances are that no one would be the wiser. Even if you do get caught, the repercussions could be mild or even non-existent. (Most likely if anyone called them on it, they'd blame it on the distributor—me!—even though I gave them exactly what they asked for.)

But it's dishonest. If you represent yourself as having only the best ingredients—and price your menu accordingly—yet deliver something to customers that is not, by definition, the best, then at the very least that's a lie of omission. It's even more dishonest when "Market Price" comes into play. If the price per pound that you pay rarely or never changes, then listing something as MP on a menu is only a plot to over-charge unsuspecting diners.

Market Price is only appropriate in very rare circumstances—when you're bringing in something really special that you can't get year round. Something you legitimately could not have priced out in advance. Say, something like razor clams or Florida Stone Crab Claws. Even then, those items should probably be listed under "Specials," because that's exactly what they are. That would be more honest and less intimidating to customers.

People in this industry—restaurants and distributors alike—some-times lose sight of the fact that there is an end-user here: the diner. I hate to admit it, but we all play a hand in lying to diners day in and day out. Sometimes it feels like we're playing Russian Roulette, just one rotation of the barrel away from the fatal headshot of the customer find-ing out the various ways his menu is lying to him.

I try to run as clean an operation as I can. We tell our customers that "what you order is what you get." We strive to make the supply chain as stable and predictable as possible, but there are still surprises in store from time to time. This product or that might not be readily available due to circumstances beyond anyone's control. If there is an availability issue, we try to give reasonable notice and go over any and all accurate pricing that reflects a standard markup. That's the honest way to do business, but you don't always see that happening. Sometimes, instead of just being straightforward like that and taking their lumps, a distributor will secretly swap in a lesser grade product. Or even worse, attempt to pass off frozen as fresh, defrosting fish in the sink of their warehouse before putting it on a truck. I don't think this kind of thing happens a lot, but it happens often enough that it's alarming and dismaying.

ANY BIG-TICKET FISH is susceptible to these types of market manipulations. Flounder, swordfish, red snapper, and King Crab are all items that you're going to be overpaying for in almost every restaurant in America. Dover sole, too, might be one of the worst offenders. I will never order this when I go out, even though it's absolutely delicious, because of its well-deserved reputation in the industry as a notorious ripoff.

It's interesting to see the effect that all the disruption of 2020 had on the worldwide seafood market. King crab went from $17 a pound to more than $40. Frozen lobster meat from Maine and Canada was sitting steady at $20 a pound and now is closer to $50. Brazilian lobster tails went from $17 a pound to more than $30. You'd think that when all the fine dining restaurants shut down—some temporarily, some for good—that the prices on these luxury items would have dipped, but just the opposite has happened. Supply is very low, and demand is high. People are suddenly buying these products hand-over-fist, maybe making up for lost time.

King crab especially is one of those items that is almost always listed as MP, probably because the sticker shock is so intense. It's not uncommon for a single order to be listed on a restaurant's menu in the $80 to $100 range, and we're talking one or two legs per order. That's barely a pound of product. When restaurants were paying less than $20 a pound for it, that already represented a hefty markup. But with prices so high as of this 2021 writing, restaurants literally can't afford to give it to diners that cheap anymore. Are diners prepared to spend $200 on a king crab dish that won't even leave them full? The rich and elite may throw money around casually, but they still have a ceiling for what they'll pay, even on a status symbol ingredient like that. Restaurants may have reached the limit on what "Market Price" will allow them to get away with. Is it possible that karma is real?

Oddly enough, a product that fluctuates wildly in price but you almost never see listed as a Market Price item is salmon. This is because restaurants have discovered that salmon is popular enough that they don't even need to do the entire MP song and dance. Salmon just sits on everyone's main entree list at a steady (and absurdly inflated) price. It's maddening, because salmon is more unpredictably priced than any other fish I know. It's constantly hitting new highs, then quickly dipping down to record lows. But the demand from diners and restaurants is still there.

Even worse, in a quest for more price stability, farmed salmon is expanding in ways that could actually start to endanger the entire supply chain. Farmed Atlantic salmon is popular enough that suppliers are starting to set up aquaculture operations in the Pacific Northwest, which has always been admired mostly for the quality of its wild salmon. Since the breed of salmon that fare best in farm environments are very different than the breeds that are found in the wild, you're starting to see people take eggs from the east coast hatcheries and attempting to transfer them to the newly-established west coast fisheries.

This mixing of populations has potentially disastrous consequences. Remember, these farms are mostly on the open ocean, with the livestock contained in netting. If one of the Atlantic-originating salmon escapes and mingles with the local population, there's the possibility they could spread a disease or parasite that could decimate the wild salmon. This might sound alarmist, but if COVID taught us anything it's that diseases that no one saw coming can lead to massive, unforeseen changes.

THE BIGGEST RUB with Market Price is that it doesn't work both ways. The price that the diner pays can always go *up* as the costs of ingredients rise. But I guarantee you that the restaurant will not charge *less* if the cost of the product dips.

That is why I'm such a big proponent of frozen over fresh. Almost across the board, no matter the product, you are better off going frozen. (Obviously, there's a fair bit of self-interest there, as frozen is a big chunk of my business. But let's put that aside for a second.) The price advantages of frozen product go without saying. Going with frozen also smooths out a lot of seasonal availability issues, and insulates you from price fluctuation. There's even a fair case to be made that in some instances, the quality of frozen *exceeds* that of "fresh."

Take scallops, for example. I love a scallop more than almost any other seafood. When we have them fresh—truly fresh, untreated, straight from the boat—in the warehouse, I'll sample the goods in the name of quality control, popping them in my mouth like they were Skittles, several times a day as I make my rounds on the warehouse floor. So believe me when I say I'm a scallop fan.

But a lot of the stuff being sold as "fresh" isn't what you imagine. The high prices on this product have led, as they so often do, to all kinds of cheating and corner-cutting. Unscrupulous suppliers or distributors will soak them in a brine composed of something called tripolyphosphate. It increases the shelf life of the product, improves the color, makes it firmer and glossier. But it also encourages the little guys to soak up water, bulking up their weight by as much as 30 percent. This is the seafood equivalent of a butcher putting his finger on the scale. Restaurants may or may not even know that the product they're advertising as fresh has been treated in this way, so they're potentially overpaying by a third on a product they're assuming is top-notch.

If the supplier overdoes it on the brine, it can truly affect the quality. Scallops are at their best when they're just lightly seared in some butter or oil, turning them golden brown on the top and bottom, while leaving them rare in the middle. The resulting contrast in textures is one of the most pure delights in the culinary world. But in a scallop that's been over-treated, there's a ton of water that has to cook off before the scallop can achieve that lovely crust, and there's a risk of them cooking through and turning rubbery before they even begin to brown.

(For you at-home chefs, there's an easy way to tell if your fresh scallops are untreated or "dry." Take a paper towel and rest the raw scallop on it for a minute or so. Then pick it up and look at what's left behind. If there's a sizable moisture ring on the towel, you know you have an inferior product. Or later, when you're cooking it, if you see a lot of milky liquid leaching from the scallop as soon as it hits the heat, and it seems like it's taking forever to get a sear, that's another telltale sign you have an overly-processed and treated scallop.)

Fresh-off-the-boat scallops are best, but I'll take a properly frozen scallop in second place over a heavily brined one any day of the week.

In most cases we should all be way more interested in frozen seafood. Product that is pulled from the water and flash-frozen on the same boat that caught it marks the beginning of a much better and more transparent supply chain. Frozen seafood tends to have better traceability, carries less disease, and is more affordable to boot. If I could have you take away one message from this book, it's this: don't turn your nose up at frozen seafood.

IRONICALLY, I THINK that fine dining restaurants could take a few cues from what the middlebrow chains are doing. I'm talking Applebee's, Chili's, and The Cheesecake Factory. One thing I admire about those chains is that they're not trying to represent themselves as something they're not. They're not lying and advertising "diver scallops" or "wild Gulf shrimp," for run-of-the-mill ingredients, because they're large and high-profile enough that they know they can't get away with it. They are transparent about their pricing, too. It's easy to mock a "2 for $20" entree special, but at least they're not ambushing customers with a hefty bill after the fact.

And that's the worst thing about Market Price to me. It's a dead giveaway that someone, somewhere in the process is looking to pull the wool over your eyes. Maybe it's the restaurant. Maybe it's the supplier, or the distributor, or even the fisherman. But the lack of transparency inherent in putting that pricing on a menu should be setting off alarm bells in your head every time you see it.

Chapter 12

KICKED IN THE TENTACLES

MY CO-AUTHOR JOE is married to a lovely woman named Jenny. She's the total package—smart, funny, beautiful, a good mother and a rising star in the world of academic publishing. She does, however, have one very large, almost irredeemable flaw.

She doesn't like seafood.

When people hear this they usually react in utter disbelief. "There's such a wide range of options available to try! Surely there's something that's appealing to you? Sushi? Lobster? Swordfish? Shrimp cocktail? Fish taco?"

Jenny just calmly explains that she doesn't like it. Any of it. She can't really explain it, either. She just doesn't.

Yes, she's tried some of it before, taken a nibble or two off someone else's plate if she was feeling a little adventurous maybe, or had a few glasses of wine in her. She's certainly aware that her food opinion is widely considered wrong; that other people love some of this food; that there's entire cultures that base most of their cuisine on ingredients from the ocean. But none of that moves her. She won't acquiesce. She's even taken to claiming that she's allergic to seafood—yes, all seafood— just to get people off her back about it.

But there's one exception to her otherwise ironclad rule against: fried calamari.

Maybe it's her Italian heritage. Or maybe no one can resist the allure of something battered, fried, salted, and dipped in marinara sauce. Either way, that's the one type of seafood she'll eat.

THERE IS NO more complicated item to sell than squid. More so than any other seafood, that cephalopod has countless varieties, countries of origin, methods of processing, and even brand names; and almost every restaurant wants something different. Squid is also the most difficult to keep consistent from catch-to-catch. This is generally a nightmare for restaurants, whose workflows require repeatability night after night.

Whether they're going to fry, stuff, grill, or simply sauté it and toss it with some pasta, restaurants want squids that are going to be the same size, texture, and taste as the last box that came into their kitchen. Because when the calamari is off, it's a lot harder to hide. Most diners can't taste the difference between red snapper and a lane snapper, for example. But they'll definitely notice when the tender calamari they enjoyed a month ago is now chewy. (By the way, I and every other squid distributor has come to dread picking up the phone and hearing the phrase "it's too chewy," because we know that the next thing the person is going to tell us is that the product is coming back to us at a loss.)

There are at least three hundred different species of squid in the ocean, but for the purposes of the food industry, there are two main ones: loligo and illex.

Loligo is better—with tender flesh and a sweet taste—and therefore more in demand, and more expensive. Illex is more affordable, thanks to a firmer, double-walled mantle (a.k.a. the head part) that's almost single-handedly responsible for squid's chewy reputation.

Squid is found all over the place, but the best specimens don't come from Italy or Japan, like you might suspect. Believe it or not, the greatest calamari in the world is caught just off the coast of Rhode Island, in the waters surrounding Point Judith, not too far from Narragansett.

If you ever find yourself in Rhode Island, do yourself a favor and try some fresh. The tentacles on these things are ounce-for-ounce maybe the most flavorful thing in the entire seafood world. I wish more restaurants would take it this way, fresh from the docks—"dirty" as we call it—before processing and shrinkage has a chance to sap its flavor and texture.

The problem is that the squid that's fresh out of the water largely does not go to restaurants outside of the state. Most of the fresh squid is used locally. I can occasionally get my hands on some, but it's rare.

It's much more common for squid to be frozen right on the boat by the fishermen. This is because there aren't that many squid-only fishermen; rather most of these guys are at sea for multiple days, and squid is just one of the things they catch. It's just not practical or cost-effective for them to head in to market every day, so the squid are put in suspended animation while the boats turn their attention to other catches.

A lot of squid gets shipped directly to Europe, because at the end of the day the Euros are willing to pay more for it. In America, squid is maybe not considered a delicacy like lobster or king crab, so diners and chefs balk at high prices. It's definitely a loss for us, because I'd put a properly-sourced, well-prepared calamari up against almost any other seafood. Grill it over a wood fire, drizzle it with a good, peppery olive oil, a light squeeze of lemon, and a touch of flaky sea salt and it's one of my favorite things in the world to eat. But the market just isn't there for it in the States, so it remains sort of a niche item.

My personal theory is that squid is so alien-looking that Americans tend to be almost scared of it. Or it's entirely possible that there's a halo effect from the dish that Americans are most used to seeing on their menus: Jenny's favorite, fried calamari. When you're conditioned to think of an ingredient as something that's on the menu for $12.99, and served in a paper-lined basket as an accompaniment to wings and beer, it's maybe hard to justify spending a lot more, even for an upscale preparation.

ONE ODDITY OF the squid market is is that even though a lot of the best in the world are caught right here in the good old US of A, they're immediately sent off to China to be cleaned, processed, and frozen before being put on a boat back to the United States.

Why does calamari take this bizarre round trip? Because the labor in China is cheap enough that the cost savings of getting product processed abroad more than make up for the shipping fees. When China sends American-caught squid our way, they also send plenty of Chinese- and Thai-caught product as well. In fact, that's now the majority of what's sold into the marketplace.

The foreign-harvested squid is not necessarily a bad product in and of itself, but it is often given a treatment that can virtually ruin it.

It's called a "glaze," and we're not talking about the kind that makes your Krispy Kremes delicious. It's a chemical cocktail that's meant to protect the delicate squid skin from oxygen and other elements that would cause it to deteriorate quickly. A little bit of glaze can be helpful, allowing the squid to hold for longer in deep freeze, preserving the color and the visual appeal. But when packaging squid, some processors go way overboard, to the point where I believe the net weight of the product is being dishonestly manipulated.

A restaurant might be paying for five pounds of squid, but in a lot of cases, once defrosted they find they're losing 15 to 20 percent of the weight. At this point, you have to realize that the quality of the product has been tampered with. Over-glazing ruins the texture and taste, making the final product seem like it's perpetually undercooked, no matter how much heat the kitchen throws at it.

I try to explain to my customers that cheaping out on calamari is not going to save them money in the long run. The per-pound price might look better on paper, but when you factor in weight loss, the supposed savings evaporate. I steer them to the less glazed product, which doesn't lose as much weight, is easier to cook, and eats so much better when it finally arrives on the diner's plate.

American-processed calamari is the gold standard, and I always recommend that to my customers. Town Dock in Narragansett and Top Catch in Brooklyn are two of my favorite domestic suppliers. The price is a little higher, sure, than the stuff coming off the boat from China. But you're going to taste exactly where that extra money went.

Let's save the glazing for donuts, people.

Chapter 13

YOU CAN BE SO SHELLFISH SOMETIMES

THE FIRST PERSON in history to eat a raw oyster must have either been starving to death or trying to win a bet.

That's the only conclusion that makes sense, from a strictly visual perspective.

Because for starters, the outside of an oyster isn't particularly enticing. It's dark and gnarled and crusty-looking. Other shellfish are much prettier. Scallops and conchs and even (to a lesser extent) clams and cockles have beautiful, geometric, otherworldly-looking shells. I can see someone being curious about what's going on inside one of those.

Oysters, by comparison, look like lumpy elongated rocks.

And once you get *inside* the oyster, the visuals get even worse. The quivering grayish-beige mass looks a lot more like snot than like anything that you'd actually want to eat. So the person that took that first bite was either very hungry, very brave, or very desperate to impress their friends.

So we know that the look isn't great. But the taste?

The taste is unreal.

Almost indescribable, really. The closest I can put it into words is, it tastes like the ocean in the best way possible. Sweet and briny with a clean mineral aftertaste.

In case you can't tell, I love raw oysters. And raw clams, for that matter. There's something so primal about slurping something down on the half shell, something that doesn't need a recipe or any cooking at all to taste good. Maybe you add a squeeze of lemon, a couple dashes of hot sauce, or a little spoonful of mignonette, but a lot of the time it doesn't need a damn thing. It's just the pure essence of the sea in a tasty little bite.

The lovely thing about eating raw shellfish is that it really lets the quality of the product shine through. You can't hide sub-par sourcing with fancy techniques or recipes. If you end up with a bum batch of oysters, all the mignonette in the world won't be able to obscure it.

Of course, it's not for culinary reasons alone that you should be careful about where you get your shellfish from. One of these suckers can literally kill you if you're not careful! The odds are small—about a hundred Americans a year die from food poisoning or infection caused by raw shellfish—but not non-existent.

Since oysters and clams are what's known as filter feeders—they suck water into their shells, skimming nutrients from it before spitting it back into their surroundings—they are especially prone to absorbing anything nasty in the environment. Bacteria, chemicals, raw sewage, or anything else wrong with the water will quickly show up in the animals faster than with any other type of seafood.

Shellfish are known to spoil quickly when mishandled, too. Since they're generally kept alive until the last possible moment before shucking or cooking, anything that kills them prematurely can make them inedible later on. They are particularly sensitive to changes in temperature, and can also be killed by something as simple as a prolonged soak in fresh water (as opposed to salt water, which is what they're used to).

For all these reasons, I choose to primarily eat oysters and clams at my home, where I know a lot of details about the sourcing, and can see the quality as I open each one, choosing which specimens make my plate and which end up in the trash.

And let me say I realize that not everyone has the luxury of being able to enjoy shellfish at home. Depending on where you live, they might be hard to source. Or you simply might be too intimidated to attempt shucking them yourself. So fear not! In this chapter we'll also talk about how to maximize your restaurant experience for what I believe is one of the most fun and pleasurable seafoods you can get.

I LIVE IN CONNECTICUT on a small farm. I don't really grow anything substantial—just some produce in a small garden for me and my wife, with enough left over to give to some friends and family. I'm surrounded by a few other farms as well: dairy, hog, vegetables, flowers. But one of the fastest-growing farm products in my state is something I could never hope to grow myself, because all the growth and harvesting takes place underwater. That's right: there are over seventy thousand acres of shell-fish farms along the coast.

These underwater farms are monitored very carefully, scrutinized by state regulators more so than any other agricultural concern in the state (possibly with the exception of the newly-legalized recreational marijuana industry). And this scrutiny is warranted, because something as simple as a heavy rain can send a torrent of runoff into the oyster beds, inundating them with bacteria and God-knows-what-else that can potentially be passed along to anyone who eats them.

That's the worst-case scenario, of course. I'm not trying to be alarm-ist. Just urging you to think really hard about whether or not that "Buck Per Shuck" $1 oyster night at your local saloon is worth it. I'm not saying that's something you need to avoid under all circumstances, but I do think that oysters are not necessarily the kind of thing you want to cheap out on, or binge eat in copious amounts like you might with chicken wings.

Flavorwise, I do believe that the greatest shellfish in the States come from the northeast—anywhere from Long Island all the way up to New England. Blue Point oysters and Quahog or Littleneck clams are some types to look out for. Some West Coast shellfish are pretty good too, like Pacific Razor clams, Kusshi oysters from Deep Bay in British Columbia, or Kumamoto oysters, which originated in Japan but today are cultivated in northern California and Washington state.

The thing that all these shellfish, East and West, have in common is that they are raised in relatively cool waters. This generally leads to smaller animals, because the water temperature slows metabolism; but it also makes for firmer, more flavorful meat.

The American southeast also has a thriving shellfish cultivation industry, but for the life of me I don't know why any restaurant outside of that immediate region would menu that product.

Compared to their hardscrabble cousins in the cold waters of the northeast and Pacific Northwest, southern shellfish have it made in the shade. Nice warm waters juice their metabolism, and there's plenty of food in the water, so they grow to some pretty impressive sizes. The animals are happy, lazy, and fat, so they certainly have a better life. But all that easy living makes the texture of their meat less firm. And the warm waters are way more susceptible to bacteria outbreaks. I personally won't eat any southern shellfish unless I'm actually on vacation down there, and even then only if I truly trust the establishment I'm eating at.

Yet I get asked for southern shellfish all the time by customers in the NYC area. I definitely understand why they're interested: the favorable growth conditions means the harvest down there is way more abundant, so the product is cheaper. Compare that to the northeast, where shellfish have to fight against the sometimes-hostile conditions. All that fighting translates to flavor, though.

Think of wine, where the *terroir* and the specific minerality of the soil and constantly-changing weather conditions means that the vine has to fight hard to produce grapes. This makes for a heartier, better-tasting grape, even if it does give the winemaker lower yields.

In the same way wine has a *terroir*, shellfish have *merroir*. Southern oysters will simply never be as good as their counterparts from colder waters, and I refuse to sell them. (Aside from taste concerns, I've also found that southern oysters simply don't keep as well. They are a lot more susceptible to dying on the long truck rides to the north. This is not as much of a problem for the battle-tested West Coast oysters, which have a lot further to travel, but a much higher survival rate.)

Believe me, my refusal to stock product from the south has caused endless headaches for yours truly. Cost-conscious restaurants beg me for southern shellfish, especially when prices of East Coast or West Coast fish spike. These spikes occur with regularity, too.

What happens is that when the aforementioned rains hit the east coast, the regulators swoop in and close all the beds. With east coast product scarce or even completely unavailable, the price of west coast shoots up. It can get to the point where west coast shellfish—already more expensive even on a good day—rises to the point where it's almost double the price of product from down south.

That's when restaurants start screaming at me about the cost. Sometimes we can fill in the gaps with shellfish from a little further north. It might be pouring in the Hamptons, for example, but if the skies are clear in Maine or Cape Cod we can get some oysters or clams from there that are a pretty close substitute. But a lot of the time even that won't work, and I end up losing the business permanently to one of my competitors who is willing to source from southern suppliers.

There is a restaurant group based in New York that presents itself as an authentic seafood shack. Even though they only have locations in Manhattan and Washington DC, they pretend that they've originated straight from the docks of a Maine coastal town. The inside is done up with all the right decor: old fishnets and nautical flags hanging from the rafters, oars mounted on the wall, worn-out wooden floorboards under-foot. They are clearly posers. The management is terrible, the food is awful, and almost nothing in their restaurant is actually from Maine. All they use are southern clams and oysters. They tried to get them from me, and I refused, so I lost not only their shellfish business but all their other business as well—shrimp, squid, and everything else.

Some C-list distributor took my place.

DESPITE PEOPLE'S FEARS, I think that the risk of food poisoning or ill-ness from shellfish is still relatively small. I even suspect that in a lot of cases, it's not that the product was bad—it's people getting sick from cross-contamination. Maybe the cutting board wasn't cleaned prop-erly, or someone used a knife on some unwashed lettuce or raw chicken before using it to shuck an oyster.

But the risk is still there. If you're eating out, the best precaution is to go to a restaurant that you trust. Ideally, the person doing the shuck-ing will be visible to you, either in an open kitchen or stationed at a raw bar set up in the middle of the dining room. When you have eyes on that person, it's an extra level of assurance that they're treating the seafood right, keeping everything on ice until service, and not accidentally cross-contaminating with other ingredients in the kitchen.

If dining at home, a quick inspection of your haul before prepping it can go a long way toward protecting yourself. The fastest way to get sick is by consuming shellfish that is dead, or even in the process of dying. Check your oysters, clams, and mussels—they should be sealed tightly before you cook or shuck them. If you see the shell hanging open a little, but clamping back shut again suddenly when you give it a tap, that's okay. That means the little guy is still alive and kicking in there. But if you see the shell gaping open, and nudging it doesn't garner a response, that thing is dead. Toss it in the trash. There's no salvaging it.

If you're baking or steaming or sautéing the shellfish, that's when you should see them finally open—once they're cooked through. If you find any that they still don't open even then, don't try to force them. Just discard those as well.

If you're eating raw, there should be a fair amount of liquid inside the shell after you shuck it. That's called the liquor. You want to preserve that, because it's delicious, so keep as much of it in the shell as you can until you slurp the whole thing down.

If, on the other hand, you shuck open an oyster or clam and there's very little liquor, or none at all, that's a bad sign. It probably means that the shellfish is in the process of dying, if not dead already. Even if you think it was alive when you started shucking, it's better to toss out these dry guys.

When in doubt, follow your nose. Shellfish that were harvested at the same time and the same place should all smell roughly the same: sweet, briny, and not remotely fishy. If you come across one that smells a bit different from its brethren, that's a red flag. If you're getting a really strong odor like low tide on the Jersey Shore, that's a flashing red light. Don't eat it.

One of the fun results of bringing home a bag of shellfish is that you sometimes find a tiny live crab or two, either scuttling around inside the bag or hiding inside one of the shellfish. Don't freak out if that happens.

It's totally normal. It doesn't mean the shellfish are bad, or contaminated. It's just that they sometimes get tiny stowaways. These are oyster crabs, also known as pea crabs. Throw it out, if you want, or—even better—fry it up in a hot pan with some butter and enjoy. You can eat it, shell and all, and it's actually considered a delicacy.

Crabs or no crabs, oysters are best within two weeks after their harvest date, provided they are properly stored and handled. They have a longer shelf life than clams, which only last a matter of days after harvesting.

And that's what you need to know about raw shellfish. Do with this knowledge what you will, and enjoy what I think is ounce for ounce one of the purest expressions of seafood.

ONCE WE'RE OUT of the realm of the raw, there's a lot more room for shenanigans.

Take the Italian restaurant standard, spaghetti vongole. Vongole, of course, is just the Italian word for "clam," but don't think that means you're getting clams from Italy. More often than not, they're using frozen white clams from China.

It's a shame, too, because there's a lot of beautiful bivalves available out there that restaurants aren't using. Cockles from New Zealand, or Manila clams from the American West Coast, for example. But those are expensive, and can suffer from availability issues. The frozen Chinese clams are as much as five times cheaper. If we've discovered anything over the course of this book, it's that if restaurants determine they can get away with using something cheaper, they'll almost never go back to using the good stuff.

In a side-by-side comparison, cockles or Manila clams would blow the Chinese clams out of the water. Even on visuals alone—the more expensive product is just prettier, with brindle coloring and rigid grooves in the shell that are so sculptural it's hard to believe that nature created it instead of an artist. The meat inside is plump and a nice size. Meanwhile, the cheaper stuff has shells that are bleached white, not nearly as pretty, with less rigid and less well-defined grooves; they come tightly packed, frozen in a layered sleeve, looking from the outside of the box more like a ream of printer paper than a natural product from the ocean. The shells contain morsels of meat that are disappointingly small.

There's no comparison on taste, either. The Chinese clams have almost a sterile taste. The flavor profile is flat, and in some cases can verge on chemical. (Have you ever had astronaut ice cream? You know how it tastes a little bit, but not quite like the real thing? Same idea here.)

Even though I love spaghetti vongole, I will rarely order it when I'm out. Unless I know the restaurant, and trust them to use good clams, I'd rather make it at home myself where I can control the quality.

This isn't a health issue—I'm not concerned that the Chinese clams are going to kill me, not in a cooked dish like vongole—but it is offensive to me that you can shell out (pun intended) upwards of $20 for an entree and get something inferior. Restaurants are banking on you not knowing the difference, and thinking what you're getting is good enough. It's trickery, and I think we should demand better of them. Otherwise they have no incentive to stop cutting corners.

Scallops are another area where you're not always getting what you paid for. You'll see a lot of menus advertising "bay scallops." This product comes from the waters around Nantucket or Long Island, and is mostly distinguished from sea scallops by size: they're a lot smaller. If you've ever had a fresh, true bay scallop you'll know how absolutely delicious they are. They don't need adornment: just some good olive oil and maybe some flakey sea salt before being tossed with some pasta.

The season for these is ridiculously short; they start cropping up in early November and are only available for two or three weeks. I look forward to this time all year. Whenever they're in the warehouse, everyone gets excited. I've told you how we'll sometimes crack open one of the gallon tubs that the scallops come in to "sample" them, which entails us all just grabbing and eating them raw throughout the course of the work day. It's not uncommon for us to make it through the entire gallon.

Due to their extreme seasonality, there's no reason why they should be on menus year round. If you order a bay scallop dish any time outside of the month of November, you're not going to get the fresh and decadent seafood you're hoping for. You're going to get a frozen imported product from Peru, or maybe somewhere in Asia that the restaurant paid $3 a pound for. Compare that to freshly harvested, in-season bay scallops that should run at least $20 to $30 a pound. (They're worth every nickel, too.)

When chefs know that we have Bay Scallops in stock, they'll call me up eager to get their hands on some. But when I give them the price—a good price, mind you, not trying to gouge anyone at all—I get screamed at. They don't want to pay what I'm asking. So they inquire about a substitute. I tell them that there's nothing that can compete. Almost always they will follow up with "do you have a tiny sea scallop that is the size of a bay scallop?" Sea scallops are good in their own right, of course, but they're not quite the same thing as bay scallops. A very small sea scallop does *look* the same as a standard-sized bay scallop, but the taste will be different. They're firmer, and not as tender and sweet.

You can bet that if they do find someone to supply them with the smaller, cheaper sea scallops the menu is still going to say "bay" and the price is going to stay high.

Chapter 14
TODAY'S SUPER SAVER SPECIAL? FOOD POISONING!

I'D RATHER EAT out of the trash than buy seafood at your average supermarket.

It sounds hyperbolic, but it's God's honest truth. As messed up as the sourcing at restaurants can be, it doesn't hold a candle to the sheer amount of fuckery that's going on at your neighborhood market.

Early on in my sales career, I tried to break into that market. What I found was a baffling mix of sweetheart deals, indifference to quality, price gouging, and open corruption.

I started with what seemed like an easy target: a small regional chain in Westchester County. It's where I grew up, so I assumed I'd have my finger on the pulse of what the local ecosystem wanted. My fellow salesmen warned me that it was a fool's errand to go after this sector, but I was young and cocky, trying to prove everyone wrong. I assumed that with my pedigree and some good old-fashioned persistence, I could land what looked like a large prize that was ripe for the taking.

I should have listened to my colleagues.

The frustration started immediately after I landed my first meeting. The guy was a buyer for five different stores. Five locations doesn't sound

141

like a lot, but by our standards it would have been a huge account, and it felt like a promising way to crack into the sector and get my feet wet.

The first thing he told me was that his chain bought exclusively from one of our competitors that was based in New England. This immediately set off alarm bells for me. The logistics were way off. Even though New England has great product, and this distributor in particular had an excellent reputation, there's no reason why they should be trucking stuff all that way when there were plenty of closer options. So already I was a little confused by the situation.

Before the meeting, the purchaser had given me a wish list of items, and told me what he was already paying for each of them. I checked everything against our prices, and the discrepancy was shocking. He was overpaying his New England distributor, and not just by a little. Usually when there's a cost savings to be had, I can offer a customer a few cents per pound. But in this case, I'd be able to save him several dollars, while still maintaining a healthy profit for myself.

So I made my pitch. I thought it was a slam dunk, frankly. I'd be able to offer the guy comparable—if not better—quality, at a huge savings to his stores. We're talking tens of thousands of dollars a year. I waited by the phone for the inevitable call telling me that we had a deal.

But I got crickets.

No calls. No emails. No texts. I tried following up and still got nothing. I couldn't even get the guy on the phone. I took to haunting the various locations, trying to catch him in person. One time he was actually on the premises, but refused to come out of the office to talk to me.

I could not figure out for the life of me what I had done wrong. Did I accidentally say something insulting about his wife? Had I smelled of B.O. at the meeting? Was he simply embarrassed that someone had marched into his office and pointed out that he was massively overpaying for product? None of it made sense.

I asked my dad what he thought. He went to one of the stores (it wasn't far from his house) and scoped out the fish case to see what kind of product we were dealing with, and asked around a little. He called me into his office the next day for his verdict.

"Allen, the only thing I can think of is that the guy is related to someone at the distributor," he said. "Either that, or he's taking a kickback."

I'd never heard of this happening before, but my dad said it was sadly pretty common. A purchaser who knows they're not getting a ton of scrutiny from their bosses will intentionally overpay a distributor, who will essentially bribe them in return. These aren't your basic low-level perks that distributors will sometimes dangle as incentives—a case of lobster tails, or some tickets to the Big Game or something. We're talking about cold hard cash: an arrangement where the purchaser gets a percentage of every dollar his company spends with the distributor.

It's a pretty serious allegation, because if true, this purchaser was not only screwing the customers that shopped at his supermarket, but he was also sticking it to his own company. And that's the kind of thing that ultimately drives up prices for every shopper, whether or not they even buy seafood.

Bear in mind this was just my dad's hunch. But I think he was on to something, because a few months later the purchaser left the company under mysterious circumstances. He apparently landed on his feet quickly, because a few weeks after that he resurfaced, this time working for another chain of stores on Long Island.

A dear friend of the family who was also a distributor happened to hold the seafood account with that chain. One day shortly after the shady purchaser took over, our friend was told that he had lost the business. There was no reason given, no chance for him to plead his case, no mention of possibly negotiating an incentive to keep the account, like cutting a break on prices.

Just *poof*, like that. A business relationship that had lasted years was gone overnight. Immediately my dad and I knew what was up. We told our friend, but of course none of us had any solid proof, just a suspicion, so there was nothing we could do.

Fast forward a couple of years, and get this—the guy got caught. His boss, the owner of the chain, finally took a long hard look at the books and realized what was happening. He confronted his employee (as we heard later from our friend, who got the whole story when the owner contacted him to re-establish their relationship) and asked him point blank: "Would you mind explaining why we are paying $2 per pound higher on everything? And why we have to wait two or three full days for a delivery from two hundred miles away, when our old distributor is right around the corner, delivers same day, and is significantly cheaper?"

The purchaser was caught red-handed and fired on the spot.

This type of business, unfortunately, is rampant, and isn't even exclusive to supermarkets. It happens at hotels, casinos, country clubs, and even in the rarefied air of Manhattan's private Ivy League alumni clubs. A few years back another guy who managed the restaurant at one of these clubs—which are clustered near Grand Central Terminal—was let go for allegedly taking kickbacks from almost every vendor he did business with.

Now whenever I pitch a potential customer who seems like a no-brainer to make the switch to my company, but don't land the account for some unexplained reason, my first suspicion is always that this type of corruption is behind it. It's sad that my mind goes there first. Maybe I'm naive, or idealistic, but it's just another harsh reality of this industry.

THE NUMBER OF sushi restaurants in the United States more than doubled between 2011 and 2021. Sushi's explosion in popularity in America in the past decade has been good for my industry, no doubt. But as with any food trend, downmarket versions that are a sad imitation of the real thing have proliferated as well.

Enter the supermarket sushi station. A lot of these places will have a chef on the premises. Usually it's an Asian person, wearing a white uniform, complete with a tall hat. But it's all for show. These supermarkets want to give you the illusion of freshness and quality, but comparing grocery store sushi to the authentic stuff served in a true, dedicated sushi bar is like pitting a White Castle slider against a grilled dry-aged porterhouse. (Actually, that's maybe unfair to White Castle, which—unlike grocery store sushi—is plenty delicious if you're high enough.)

A real sushi restaurant carefully sources their fish, and is meticulous about storing and preparing them. They labor over their rice, obsessing about the perfect ratio of vinegar, salt, and sugar to add to it. They generally close for a few hours every day at 2:30 p.m., turning away anyone looking for a late lunch in favor of prepping properly for that evening's dinner service. They have almost nothing else on their menu besides sushi—no chicken teriyaki or ramen or sake bombs. When they make a piece of nigiri, they serve it to you immediately, with the rice still a little warm. They offer you good aged soy sauce and real wasabi—freshly grated from the authentic Japanese-grown root—as accompaniments.

Compare that to the supermarket sushi. The fish is likely to be clumsily defrosted, inexpensive frozen tuna-loin from Indonesia, or imitation crab meat made from nondescript fish that's been pressed into a cake. The rice is under-seasoned and formed into hard clumps. The food is made in the morning, loaded into plastic clamshell containers, and piled into a refrigerated display case. The accompaniments are generic packets of soy sauce, and globs of thick, pasty imitation wasabi made of horseradish, mustard powder, and green food coloring. And, most damning, even at the places with a chef on the premises, most of the sushi you can grab has been sitting for hours, where the refrigeration wreaks havoc on the taste and texture of the fish.

The sushi station at a supermarket is emblematic of their approach to seafood as a whole. They put on a big show of being committed to quality, but as soon as you start digging into the details the whole thing falls apart.

In fact, head over to the larger seafood case at any big grocery store and what you'll find is absolutely disgusting: previously frozen cod that's been just left out to defrost; tuna steaks that were filleted in Asia before being shipped around the world; pre-peeled, pre-cooked shrimp, wrongly-labeled as "jumbo" but no bigger than your pinky finger; and squid that's been, inexplicably, breaded.

I've fielded dozens of calls over the years from friends or family members who are standing at the fish counter in their local grocery store, frozen with indecision. "Allen, I'm just trying to make shrimp scampi tonight, and the only thing they have is something that's pre-peeled, pre-cooked, sized 16/20, and $19.99 a pound. Is that the right thing to get? Is that even a good deal?" (For the record: no, and no.)

Americans want more control over their diets, and cooking at home is a great way to do that. Seafood is one of the healthiest things you can eat, but the main source for it in most neighborhoods is completely dysfunctional. Seafood is the last of the wild frontiers when it comes to the culinary world. Even with regulations supposedly in place, the enforcement is pretty toothless, and much of the trillion-dollar global industry is still spared from any scrutiny.

Things are much better in Europe, where the regulations are tighter, and the standards of the customers are much higher. The quest for quality is embedded in the culture over there, and massive supermarkets that carry every type of ingredient are still sort of a foreign concept to much of the continent. They're much more likely to go to separate shops that specialize in the ingredient they're looking for: the fishmonger, the butcher, the cheese shop, the bakery.

Here in the states, we're more interested in mass consumption and convenience. When was the last time you went to a standalone fishmonger? When was the last time you even saw one in your neighborhood, for that matter? The selection you get from a dedicated shop is far superior, and the expertise of the people behind the counter blows away that of your average grocery store worker. We are a country that supposedly trusts experts. You wouldn't buy a car, or a computer, or any other big-ticket item from someone who knew nothing about it. But when it comes to a decision about what we put in our bodies, we're content to seek out no further information than whatever is written on the little cards in the display case. Making multiple stops while shopping for food is anathema to many Americans, and this has hurt our ability to consume quality goods, get educated about what we eat, and make good decisions about how to spend our money.

A lot of supermarkets do try hard, especially the smaller, independent ones. Keep an eye out for places like Grace's Marketplace or Agata & Valentina, both on Manhattan's Upper East Side; or Caraluzzi's, a small chain in Connecticut. These markets do pay meticulous attention to detail, and I'd trust them for any seafood they sell.

A couple of the big chains do seem committed to doing things right as well—Whole Foods, Costco, and H-Mart (a chain of Korean-American megamarts with 84 locations across the country, mostly concentrated on the coasts and in big cities) are particularly good, I've found, so if that's your only option that's a decent bet. But I maintain that going to smaller local specialty shops is always going to give you the best results.

SHOPPING AT GROCERY stores for your seafood can be risky because of how often they blatantly lie about some of their items.

I was in a store not too long ago and they had what was listed as "fresh tuna steaks." These steaks were perfectly uniform, bright ruby-red, with no variance in color or texture whatsoever. That's a bit of a red flag, because that kind of uniformity is rare with something that occurs in nature, and is often an indication of some shenanigans during processing. So right away my antennae went up, and I decided to take a closer look. I examined the little info card mounted on the shelf of the refrigerator case, and sure enough all the way at the bottom in little tiny baby letters it said "previously frozen." Good on them I guess for admitting it, but it was still problematic that in much larger letters above they'd also written "FRESH." This mixed message was a little misleading (probably intentionally so), but I guess they figured that they were being transparent enough that their dishonesty would be forgiven. Of course, it would have been better if they'd kept the product frozen and let the customers do the thawing themselves, but maybe they thought it would be more convenient for people to buy something that was ready to cook immediately. The real problem here was that these previously-frozen tuna steaks that had probably cost the store roughly $6 a pound were being sold at a fresh markup: $23 per pound. The price was an outrage; at a reputable fish monger, this would get you top-quality, fresh #1 tuna in a whole loin (which we know is superior to pre-cut steaks).

Someone had clearly put a lot of thought into the trickery, intentionally mislabeling and misleading, while still giving themselves plausible deniability with a tiny note on the placard that most shoppers would miss. It was something that had taken a fair amount of effort. If only the department manager had put the same effort into sourcing a better product in the first place, or at least educating the customers on what they were about to buy.

The stores' fear, I think, is that if they give customers a peek behind the curtain, the customers won't like what they see. But I've always found that more information makes for more engaged and higher-spending consumers. Maybe the store would actually make more money if they asked their local distributor to come in on a Saturday and do a demo or something, one where they explain to customers why frozen tuna can be just as good, especially for the price.

But there are billions of dollars at stake in the industry, and the quicker and easier route to grabbing some of that money is by lying. That is the sad reality.

Stores could also stand to spend some time educating their employees. Then maybe there'd be more counter workers who are familiar with the products and can speak about them honestly, guiding people down the right path toward culinary excellence.

Even more so than dishonesty or ignorance, my issue with supermarket seafood is their complacency. Oftentimes they simply don't care where their product comes from. As long as it looks good in the display case, nothing else matters.

A few years back, one of our suppliers offered us ten thousand pounds of shrimp that had, through some twist of fate, been sitting forgotten in cold storage for three years. Whether it was a paperwork mishap, or a return gone wrong, this shrimp was suddenly on the market well past its sell-by date.

It might surprise you when I tell you that it's not illegal to sell seafood like this. As long as it's been continually frozen the whole time, the USDA considers it safe to eat indefinitely. Realistically, the taste and texture starts to go south after something like six months to a year, depending on the specific product, but even after that it's still not going to kill you.

Keep in mind, this was #1 wild shrimp. It had been, at one point, the best available. And it was being offered to us at $5 a pound cheaper than the going rate. The supplier was willing to sell it at a massive loss, because they just wanted it off their hands. They didn't want to parcel it out to a bunch of different distributors either—they just needed someone to take the whole load and be done with it. We crunched the numbers, and discovered that if we wanted to flip it, we'd be able to easily clear something like $50K to $75k in pure profit.

It would have been a huge score, and we heavily considered it. We took a few sample cases and thawed them to see what we were dealing with. And it actually defrosted and cooked up okay, even after three years in suspended animation. But we knew if we tried to sell it, we were playing with fire. This was a heavily compromised version of one of our flagship products, a product that was supposed to be perfect in every way. Dumping something like that on the market could spook our customers and taint future sales for years down the line. It just wasn't worth it in the end, and we passed on the deal.

A week later I heard that a grocery chain had taken the entire she-bang, at an even cheaper price than we had been offered. Did they even realize what they were getting into? The dating information on seafood is sometimes intentionally vague. Instead of printing a clear, easy-to-read "this product was processed on this date"-type statement on each case, the true date is obfuscated with a series of numbers that references the fishing season. You practically need a decoder ring to read this gibberish, and once you figure out what it says, it's still not giving you that much information, or an actual date. It might tell you something like, "Caught on the 5th vessel run of the 7th day of the season" or "packed on the 9th run of the warehouse on the 3rd day of the season." It's confusing even for a seasoned hand, and for a grocery store buyer who isn't necessarily used to dealing directly with suppliers, it could be something they'd overlook entirely.

Are you willing to take that risk when buying seafood? I'm certainly not.

I am not telling you that you need to buy the best quality at the highest price from the most expensive store you can find. But you should never feel confused, or frustrated, or anxious when buying seafood. You should know exactly what you're buying, and be confident you're getting it at a fair and reasonable markup. You might not be the richest person in the world, but that does not mean that you shouldn't be able to access good quality, delicious, fresh ingredients.

So my best advice to you would-be at-home chefs: when you have a hankering for cooking up some scallops or a nice sea bass fillet, do yourself a favor and find a local, knowledgeable fishmonger that has a good reputation. Even if you have to go out of your way to shop there, you're going to have a wider selection, more reasonable prices, higher quality, and ultimately a much better meal.

Chapter 15
COVER GIRL

I REALLY DON'T want to ruin lobster for you guys. I promise I don't. Because I for one, love it. I love it so much that I put it on the damn cover of this book! And when lobster is done right, steamed or boiled whole, served with little dishes of melted butter and a variety of shell-cracking tools and even a cute little bib, it's not only one of the tastiest seafoods to eat but also one of the best overall dining *experiences* you can have.

So I'm going to tread carefully.

What we need to talk about is the lobster that you're *not* eating directly out of the shell. It gives me no pleasure to tell you that unless you are personally picking the meat from the lobster yourself, chances are you are not getting fresh lobster meat. You are getting it frozen.

Lobster is a little bit the victim of its own success here. The demand is off the charts these days. Once restaurants discovered that diners are okay with paying high prices for lobster, they found that a great way to boost their margins is to start putting lobster meat in otherwise ho-hum dishes. That's how we get lobster ravioli, lobster mac-and-cheese, lobster risotto, lobster burgers, and—yes, everyone's favorite—the lobster roll.

Ideally, every time you order one of those dishes, the kitchen would be harvesting a live lobster for you. But this doesn't happen for a couple reasons. For one, it's just not convenient for kitchens to keep live lobsters around at all times. Having live lobsters is a little bit like having pets. You can't neglect them, or they will die. (Sometimes, even if you don't mistreat them, they actually just conk out and go to sleep. They're alive, but seem dead enough that I'll get an angry phone call from a chef who thinks I just sold him a crate of deceased crustaceans. When the crate returns to the warehouse the next day, those lobsters are all dancing around like they just escaped prison, which I guess in a way they did.)

Another reason live lobsters aren't always viable for busy restaurants is the amount of time and labor they entail. It's very difficult for a kitchen in the middle of a dinner rush to justify taking the effort to steam or boil a lobster, then ice it down, crack it all open, and harvest the meat.

Cost is actually not as much of an issue as you think it might be. The price does fluctuate, but when they are in season, live lobsters can get surprisingly cheap. I told you earlier about that time a decade ago when it was selling for barely over a dollar a pound. We haven't seen prices like that recently, but it's not unusual in a regular year for the per pound cost to dip under $4 a pound. Depending on the time of year, it can actually be one of the most economical ingredients in the entire kitchen.

But even with the price low at times, it's still not viable for a restaurant to rely on live creatures when they need it year round. So they turn to an easier, more convenient, more stable-cost option: frozen, pre-picked lobster meat.

Now these products are not bad. They're like any other frozen seafood—as long as the lobster is processed, cleaned, and flash-frozen with care, as close to the harvesting time as possible, the meat can still potentially be as delicious as fresh.

This product generally ships from Canada, where the big processing factories are. It might assure you to know that it is plucked by hand. (They still haven't invented a machine that's as efficient at extracting lobster meat as skilled humans are.) The pickings are vacuum-packed before being frozen and sent all over the world to people like me.

It's labeled by what part of the lobster it came from. Claw & Knuckle meat (CK) is the best and most desirable. Claw, Knuckle, and

Leg (CKL) is a little cheaper. Bringing up the rear is "broken" meat, which is whatever other loose scraps they could harvest from the carcass.

As always, restaurants love to play games with what they serve you. They'll mix and match the different types of meat as needed. Maybe they throw a claw or two into that lobster salad just for show, but pad out the rest of it with broken meat and a shit ton of mayo. Not the worst thing in the world to dine on, but a potentially dishonest sleight of hand.

Again, I'm not trying to scare you away from frozen lobster meat. There's a ton of it on the market, and plenty of it is good. I'm merely warning you that your menu—as you surely know by this point in the book—is yet again potentially lying to you.

Not to harp on the old Market Price *bete noire* again, but it really rankles me when I see a lobster roll listed on a menu next to "MP." Since most of these use frozen meat, where the cost barely budges, I can only assume it's the old trick of hiding the true price from the diner. And will the menu admit the nitty gritty details of the ingredients? Of course not! Instead, it's going to say "fresh Maine lobster roll" when the meat is definitely not fresh, and might not even be from Maine. So why are you paying inflated costs when the price they paid for the product is stable year-round, and the hardest thing the chef had to do was run a bag under some cool water to thaw, then open it with some scissors?

Playing fast and loose with promising "fresh" lobster is bad enough, but at least they're serving you actual lobster. Some restaurants aren't even doing that.

During the pandemic, especially, when supply chains were messed up and frozen lobster was temporarily unavailable, people were cheating all over the place. A chef called me one day and asked me what the hell he was supposed to use for his lobster mac and cheese, one of the most popular (and expensive) items on his menu.

I suggested that he bite the bullet and use live lobster for a week or two, just to tide him over until frozen was available again. He shot me down on the spot and asked me to send him some crawfish and langostino, enticed by the idea that each of them were $10 to $15 less per pound than he'd been paying for the real deal.

(Langostino is also known as a "squat lobster" but resembles a prawn more than anything else. Genetically, it's actually a close relative of the hermit crab, which sounds grosser than it is. The meat isn't bad, but it definitely isn't what we think of as "lobster," despite the name. A few years back, Long John Silver's got a warning from the Federal Trade Commission for selling "buttered lobster bites" that were actually made from langostino. The FTC was concerned that the TV commercial announcing the new product used images of actual lobsters coming off the boat in Maine, which the government watchdog agency considered deceptive advertising. The $2.99 price probably should have already tipped off most customers that they weren't getting the real thing, but I'm sure a lot of people were fooled. I've got to hand it to Long John's though—that's a fair pricing, which is more than I can say for the chef who's using the same product but charging $31 a serving for his lobster mac.)

Getting deceived by lobster meat out of the shell is one thing. But some restaurants are taking it a step further and tricking their diners with meat *in* the shell.

Well . . . not *the* shell. *A* shell, rather. If you've ever seen something like a stuffed lobster, or maybe lobster salad that comes to your table in the hollowed-out carcass of a lobster, you might think that you're seeing proof that it was the kitchen that had produced that carcass.

But that's not always the case. Empty lobster shells are easily procured at about $1 per pound. Restaurants will take those empty shells and fill them with whatever they want.

There's a popular downtown New York restaurant that does this all the time. Their diners think they're getting fresh lobster meat served on the half shell, but what they're really getting is a frankenlobster, pulled together from frozen meat and tossed into an empty casing. Customers pay dearly for the privilege, and are none the wiser. This restaurant is owned by a well-known group that I actually had to stop selling to not that long ago. They were horrible about paying their bills, abusive to me and my staff, and stopped caring about the quality of their ingredients as soon as I made it clear that their days of easy credit were coming to an end.

None of this dishonesty changes the fact that lobster remains delicious. Sure, it's maybe a bit overexposed at this point, with every high-end or even middle-end restaurant tossing a lobster roll—or something ridiculous like lobster nachos—onto their menus as a signal to their customers that the joint is *luxurious* and *classy*.

I'm not saying that you should always avoid these types of dishes, but just be careful about where you order them from. It's an ingredient that I believe deserves to be treated with respect and honesty; you should be confident that the venue that serves it to you feels the same way I do.

We've come a long way from the days when cheap, abundant lobster was considered a "poor man's food" and forced on prisoners and servants in New England. For better or worse, lobster is considered a luxury item now. But when you do order it, keep in mind its humble roots, and be wary of anyone who tries to glam it up too much.

The Platonic ideal of a lobster meal is not in a white tablecloth dining room, but dockside in New England, maybe in sight of the boats that caught it, sitting at a picnic table with a plastic bib around your neck. If you stray from that ideal and do decide to order it in more upscale environs, just keep your wits about you and resign yourself to the fact that you may not be getting the best value.

And, as always, don't be afraid to ask questions about its origins. And if the waiter or chef can't—or won't—answer your questions?

Well, in that case, with all due apologies to my cover model . . . maybe go for the chicken instead.

Chapter 16
AFTER-DINNER DRINKS

FINANCE GUYS LOVE to talk about "diversified portfolios."

I get the rationale behind that strategy: don't put all your eggs in one basket. No doubt it's tempting to dump the entirety of your kids' college fund into a cryptocurrency named after your favorite anime character. But if you do that and VegetaCoin suddenly tanks, how are you going to tell little Timmy that the only school where you can afford now is an online university based in one of the former Soviet states? So it makes sense what the finance guys say: diversify.

I'm not a finance guy, of course. I'm a fish salesman. But maybe I won't be forever. I'm not saying I'm going to quit anytime soon, but who knows what the future will bring? There's climate change to worry about; the rise of plant-based imitation seafood; or, hell, maybe the USDA will just decide to flip-flop the food pyramid yet again and advise everyone that seafood is terrible, and we should all be eating as many trans-fats as we can shove into our mouths.

It's not *likely*; but it's *possible*. And if people suddenly stop eating fish and start eating margarine by the handful, I'd be screwed.

That's why I've been branching out into other fields.

IN 2010 I started Winchell Mountain Coffee with my longtime friend Willis Rivkin.

Just like I come from a seafood family, Willis comes from a coffee family. His dad Bob is the master roaster for Schapira's Coffee, a wholesaler in Pine Plains, New York. This company has an incredible history, going back more than one hundred years.

Schapira's has a great product, but back in 2010 they had no direct-to-consumer business, and no online presence to speak of. It was entirely wholesale. It was a good company, and profitable, but Willis and his father knew that it could be so much more.

So Willis decided to bring in the best salesman he knew: a young go-getter by the name of Allen Ricca.

I've known Willis since high school, and we'd always been kicking around the idea of going into business together. Forming a new brand to sell the coffee that his family roasted seemed like a perfect opportunity.

I was looking for a new apartment at the time, so Willis and I got a place together, all the better to work on our baby at whatever odd hours we could find. We decided to name the company after a peak not far from where Willis' dad roasted his beans: Winchell Mountain Coffee was born.

We started selling at farmers markets. Since we both still had day jobs to take care of during the week, hitting farmers markets on weekends provided a perfect opportunity to sell face to face. We were able to deal directly with potential customers, answer their questions, hand out samples, and explain what made our product different. We would wake up very early on Saturdays and Sundays and drive—sometimes for several hours—to different locations in the tri-state area. It was hard work, but it was a lot of fun.

We scored a few early victories, becoming the supplier for all of Vassar College, and getting our product on the shelves at the well-regarded Hudson Valley grocery chain Adams Fairacre Farms.

The real breakthrough for our company, though, came from an unlikely source. We got a major helping hand from one of the most talented, prolific, beloved children's book authors and illustrators alive today: Sandra Boynton.

If you have a child under five years old, you know Sandy. If you've been in a greeting card shop in the past thirty years, you probably know her as well. Her colorful animal illustrations and clever rhymes have sold over seventy-five million books, and more than half-a-billion—yes, BILLION—greeting cards since the early 1970s.

Anyway, Sandy just happened to be a family friend to the Rivkins. When Willis told her he was going into business on his own, she was excited and asked how she could help.

Coincidentally, at the time, we were discussing revamping our packaging. We'd been using very simple, minimalist bags for the coffee, just glossy black with a small Winchell Mountain logo. *But what if we could pep them up a bit? What if we could add some animals drawn by one of the most famous and successful illustrators in the world?*

When we asked Sandy if we could use some of her drawings on our labels, she enthusiastically agreed. (It turned out she'd been casually kicking the idea around with Bob for several years, but they'd never gotten around to collaborating. Starting Winchell Mountain was the kick in the pants everyone needed.) She quickly drew us up some samples—one was a wide-eyed rooster, looking like he'd been given an electric shock. That became the label for our "Wide Awake" blend. Another drawing showed a smiling, very alert cartoon cat. That was "Overdrive Espresso." My personal favorite showed a sleepy-looking hippo sitting at a table, staring at the mug of coffee in front of him. In classic Boynton style, she came up with the excellent name: the "Not A Morning Person" blend.

Our business arrangement would change later on, but in those early days Sandy actually let us use those drawings for free. As our company grew more and more, we formalized the arrangement, and now she gets a cut of every bag we sell with one of her characters on it. Even though it eats a little bit into our profits, Sandy's contribution has been indescribably valuable, a huge boon to the company, and quite probably the most important business deal I've ever put together and managed. She has a large, dedicated fan base who love to buy anything with one of her drawings on it. When we formally announced our collaboration, she posted it on social media, and we were inundated with so many orders in such a short time that we had to enlist friends and family to help us pack and ship them all.

In the last year especially, my relationship with Sandy has gone from a warm business collaboration to one of actual friendship, personal enjoyment, and admiration. She is one of the most gifted writers/musicians/artists/designers/creative minds that I have ever met. She's also quite funny—which is to be expected for such a prolific creator of funny greeting cards and quirky kids' books—and she's even funnier in person than you can imagine.

But the one thing I remain in constant awe of is her knack for business. She is—by far—one of the smartest business people I have ever had the great fortune to talk to. She is an extreme workaholic, yet is still the most generous person in the world with her time, which is quite tight as you can imagine. I thought I knew it all before I met her, but it's impossible to convey the sheer amount of new, helpful things I've learned about business while working on this project with her. All these years later, she is still working her tail off for us and for herself, because she loves what she does. She says she has no plans of slowing down, quite the opposite actually! She remains a wonderful friend, and a giant in the business world.

But just because we sell our coffee in whimsical bags, don't think that we aren't a serious coffee company. In the early years, Bob Rivkin did all our roasting. But he was itching to retire, so he taught his son everything he knew. Willis has become a master roaster in his own right. He truly inherited his father's skillset.

I love to watch him fire up our beautiful, old propane-fueled Probat brand roasters that date back to the 1950s. They're built like tanks, and run better than anything you can buy brand-new today. Obviously with technology that old, there's no digital bells and whistles, no computers controlling them or anything. Willis just uses his eyes, and his nose, and a whole bunch of knowhow to make sure the beans achieve the proper level of roasting. (The margin for error on this is smaller than you might think. You really need to pay attention and be on the ball. Willis likes to say that the difference between a light roast and French roast is about fifteen seconds; the difference between a French roast and the even darker Italian roast is another five seconds; and the difference between an Italian roast and calling the fire department is another ten seconds.)

Willis's skill has only improved over the years, and today I can confidently say that our coffee is better than anything else you will ever brew.

IN 2018, HUNTING around for yet another business to sink my teeth into, I decided that what Val's Ocean Pacific needed more than anything, was to get a little tipsy.

We needed an alcohol division.

It was an area of business I'd long been interested in getting into. The big vision was that since we already had these relationships with so many high-end restaurants selling them high-end seafood, why not also sell them something that every classy establishment can always use more of: booze!

Alcohol is also a higher margin business. With seafood, on a good day, you're lucky to clear 15 percent margins. But with something like wine importing, you can easily and routinely pull something like 30 percent to 45 percent, or even higher.

I put together a team to seek out some candidate companies that would be ripe for acquisition. The mission was to look for something that was small and well-established, but not necessarily thriving. I didn't want a failing company, mind you. I wanted something with a sound business model, and a good balance sheet, but maybe one that needed a little extra help to get to that next level.

I wanted a project, basically. Something I could really dive into and retool in my own vision. (Some guys in their thirties turn to woodworking or lawn care to fill their time; I'd much rather have a hobby that makes me money.)

After weighing a few operations that didn't pan out, we came across a little company in Connecticut called Village Wine Imports. We immediately liked the owner, a laid-back guy named Mike, and he seemed like he was very interested in selling. He had been in business for twenty years, focusing on importing from small, lesser-known, hidden gem wineries in France, Italy, and Spain, most of them family-run farms and vineyards. Over the years, Mike's portfolio had grown to about 125 different wines, and since he lived in Europe year-round, he personally scouted almost every winery he worked with, really digging into their operations and sampling as much of the goods as his liver would allow him.

Another attractive thing about Village Wine was that they had established their own private labels, including their flagship VRAC wine.

The name VRAC is a reference to the phrase "*en vrac*", which roughly translates to "bring your own bottle." (It's a tradition in many small French villages for people to get their wine by bringing bottles or jugs to the winery and filling them straight from the tapped barrels.) VRAC had been a growing brand for about a decade, mostly thanks to the popularity of its rosé varietal, the best-selling iteration of which was a three-liter box.

Now boxed wine has long gotten a bad rap, and I understand why. Traditionally in America, boxes have been reserved for the cheapest stuff, so it's no wonder so many people associate the box with crappy wine. But there's been a trend in the last decade or so of selling better wines in boxes, and VRAC was one of the labels leading the way on that. This is no cheapie wine from a random commercial vineyard in California. It's the real deal, straight from a winemaker in Provence. He makes the rosé at a vineyard that's been in his family for centuries, a beautiful estate that Woody Allen used to shoot scenes for his movie *Magic in the Moonlight* a few years back.

When I took over the company, my first order of business was hiring new sales and marketing people, and implementing some slick custom sales and inventory software. Once that was taken care of, we took a long hard look at packaging. I personally hated the look of the box, but the sales numbers didn't lie. It was clear that customers loved the convenience of buying a larger container of wine that (thanks to a vacuum-sealed dispenser bag inside) stayed fresh for weeks. The question was, how to give them that same experience in a more aesthetically pleasing way?

The solution we came up with was simple—all the real advantages of boxed wine came not from the box, but from the bag inside of it. *So let's sell just the bag!*

The new packaging looked kind of like a giant Capri Sun juicebox, but it was undeniably better-looking than the box. It really popped, standing out on the wine store shelves and distinguishing our brand as offering something unique. We found that another advantage was that the malleable pouch was a lot easier to fit in a cooler, and wouldn't get soggy sitting on top of melting ice, like the old cardboard packaging would have. The product especially took off in places like Vermont, Maine, and Colorado, as avid outdoorsmen discovered that they were perfect for hiking or boating. And in environmentally-conscious locales like New York or San Francisco, people told us that they appreciated the eco-friendliness of light, cardboard-free packaging.

The next year, building off that success, we rolled out a mini pouch, an individual 250-ml serving of rosé. Those became a hit too!

Village Wine is a cool company to run, because it gave the entire team at Val's Ocean Pacific a new problem to tackle. I find that projects like this give fresh energy to everyone involved: the seafood sales people, the warehouse crew, the drivers—everyone. It's good for morale, too because it shows the employees that the company is moving forward, and it challenges them to keep up their pace to match it.

I WAS RAISED BY normal people. Yes, we had money, but my sister and I were taught that this didn't make us special. It was instilled in us that no matter what, we were supposed to do the right thing, and care about people. This has always been my guiding light in business. By looking after my employees on all sides of the table, I have not only improved the health of my business, but improved people's livelihoods—something I take tremendous pride in.

Success in business is not preordained by any means, but it's not a mystery either. It takes hard work, attention to detail, the ability to recognize and follow up on good ideas, and the careful management of people. But if you keep those principles in mind, you're not limited to succeeding in just a single field. You can excel in any industry you decide to get into.

Chapter 17
WRAPPING IT UP TO GO

OKAY, HERE'S THE part where I drop the realest of the real knowledge on you. There's a cheat code for ordering seafood in a restaurant. With a lot of ingredients, you're really rolling the dice. You don't know in advance if you're getting something good, or crappy. You don't know if you're getting ripped off or a great value.

But there's a small list of dishes that are almost surefire bets. These aren't the most well-known entrees, or the trendiest. They're definitely not going to be the most expensive items on the menu. But they are the most consistently good. They will be excellent almost every single time you order them.

Halibut
Branzino
Skate wing
Monkfish
Fish collars
Mussels

If you see one of those on a menu, you can feel safe ordering it. The product that's out there is just a higher-caliber. With strong, stable supply chains, these fish are much less prone to the tampering and obfuscation that we see with some other ingredients.

Another way to assure you're getting the best: any time you have the option of getting the whole fish served to you, do it. That fish will be fresher and tastier than you can imagine. That fish will not have been swapped out for other mystery ingredients, unbeknownst to you. When you get the whole fish, that's the purest, most unadulterated form of seafood you can eat.

Another thing to look out for—and pounce on whenever you see it—is restaurants that instead of a set menu, have a rotating whole fish special, based on whatever the latest seasonal catch is. I've found that Greek restaurants in particular are the best at this. This is when you get the semi-obscure fish that might not be available all the time, but are fantastic in both value and taste: pompano, scorpion fish, and orata are a few that you'll thank me for recommending if you ever get a chance to try.

A FEW MORE TIPS for getting the best possible restaurant experience:

Avoid putting your whole order in at once. Even if you know every dish you want the moment you sit down, it's best to not give it all to the waiter at the same time. If you want to order drinks and appetizers all at once, that's fine. But always put off your entree orders until later. If you're not in a rush, I'd even recommend waiting until they drop the appetizers. Some kitchens have trouble properly coursing out a meal. If you order everything at once, you might get appetizers only minutes before your entrees come, plates piling up on the table like a multi-car highway wreck, and the cadence of the nice meal is ruined. The point of a meal in a restaurant isn't just to eat—it's to have a whole *experience*. Timing counts for a lot. Marathon eating is not fun.

Sometimes the server will pressure you to order everything at once. You see this a lot at shared plate–style establishments, like tapas restaurants. One of the true pleasures of this type of restaurant is the slow trickle of plates to the table, and I don't always trust the kitchen to pace it properly. So I always tell the server "if you want the order all at once that's fine, but you cannot rush us and you need to make sure it is properly coursed."

If you still don't trust them to space out the dishes enough, you could always under-order the first time around. Say you know you want ten dishes for the table. When the waiter asks you for your whole order, just name six of those dishes. Then, when the plates start coming out, put in for the remaining four. It's a good way to control the flow of the meal.

A GOOD SHORTCUT TO judge a restaurant is to look at their wine list. When you look at it, you're not looking at the prices, or the vintages. That might be something you deeply care about, and more power to you if so. But for most of you that don't have a ton of wine knowledge, there's an easy way to open the wine list and tell at a glance if the restaurant cares about your dining experience: whether or not they're selling half-bottles.

I know it may seem insignificant, but by having 375ml half-bottles on their list it shows the restaurant's ability to be nimble enough to make sure their diners have options that keep them happy. By not being totally focused on forcing you to buy a full bottle, it shows that they have other things on their mind besides just milking you for more money. It's an indicator of attention to detail, something that most likely will translate into the quality of the food as well.

Of course, bringing your own wine is always an option. It's a little bit of a power move, and servers don't always like to see it. To them, it just represents a shrinking tip. I always address it head-on and explain that it's nothing against their wine list: *I just have a bottle I've been wanting to try alongside your delicious food. I'll happily pay the corkage fee, and, by the way, this will have no impact on your tip. At the end of the meal, I'm still going to tip you out as if I'd ordered the bottle from you.*

Another way I soften the blow: bring an additional bottle, and tell your server it's for the staff after hours. *"This is for you guys when us monsters finally get out of your hair."* Same thing goes for any unfinished wine, whether a bottle you brought yourself, or one you ordered from them, especially if either is an expensive or rare one. If you don't knock off the entire bottle, make sure to tell the server you "expect the wait staff to finish it off." (Chances are they were going to do this anyway, with or without your permission, but I think they appreciate knowing that you're okay with it.)

I LOVE SUSHI. BUT it can be one of the most confusing and intimidating dining out experiences you can have. The cuisine is so popular now that you're seeing it pop up in places where it probably shouldn't be, like convenience stores or gas stations. Or restaurants that serve completely unrelated types of food. I love Chinese food and Thai food, but in my mind those restaurants should not be attempting sushi as some kind of afterthought to their moo shu pork or pad thai.

I have a few rules on where I'll get my sushi. These might seem overly-fussy to you, but good sushi is enough of a splurge meal that I want everything to be *just so* if I'm dropping that kind of cash.

First of all, if I don't know the place well, I like to call ahead and ask if they are Japanese-owned. That's not to say that people of other nationalities can't do sushi well, but there's no denying that the culture where it originated still does it best.

If you feel too weird or awkward asking that over the phone, I get it! That is sort of a weird and awkward thing to ask. A good way to *sneakily* find out is to check the operating hours. A Japanese-owned sushi joint will always close for a few hours in the afternoon, taking a decent break between lunch and dinner service. If the place is open all day, avoid it. Even better are sushi bars that don't open for lunch at all, focusing on dinner only. That's when you know the level of care they put into the food is going to be top-notch.

Another good indicator of a quality sushi place is whether or not they're BYO alcohol. Most of the time, BYO is annoying, but I find that for sushi specifically, it goes hand-in-hand with good food. It's a sign that they don't give a shit about trying to sell you booze; they just wanna give you the best possible culinary experience.

Avoid places with crazy stunt rolls, or gimmicky, pun-filled names for dishes on the menu. That is not a serious establishment. Rolls are great, don't get me wrong, but the ones laden with twenty ingredients and named after a 1950s Japanese movie monster are not exactly scream-ing authenticity. Look instead for handrolls, or simple maki with just a few ingredients. Avoid anything smothered in spicy mayo or other sauces. The pleasure of sushi is the subtle interplay of quality fish and perfectly-textured and seasoned rice. Copious toppings are just a distraction.

Same goes for gimmicky presentations. If your sushi platter comes out on a wooden boat with "smoke" from dry ice seeping out, or sparklers, that isn't authentic. Fun, maybe. But not authentic.

When I lived in Tribeca, there was a restaurant nearby called Ninja. Their gimmick was that the space was built out to resemble a sort of Japanese mountain village with fake stone-walls and little individual dining nooks that resembled dungeons. All the waiters were dressed as—you guessed it—ninjas. It was weird, and theatrical (some of the waiters yelled martial arts phrases at you when delivering dishes, or performed magic tricks between courses) and actually kind of an entertaining night out in a kitschy sort of way. But when the bill dropped and you realize you spent $100 per person on sushi that was mediocre at best, it felt a lot less entertaining.

Ninja was also large, chaotic, and bustling. Much better to look for a small, calm, and quiet sushi place. One of my favorites—which sadly shuttered during the pandemic—was Tomoe Sushi in downtown Manhattan, which barely fit fifteen customers at a time. Just a bar with a few seats and a handful of tables. That, or even smaller, is the ideal.

Case in point: Sushi Noz —Manhattan's current raw fish hotspot— has two small rooms with counter-seating only. One seats eight people, the other only seven. They do two seatings a night. (How can they survive, you might ask, serving only thirty diners a day? Easy—the omakase prix fixe menu costs either $225 or $395 per person, before alcohol.)

The best sushi chefs are very proud—some might say egotistical — people. Normally, I'm turned off by that, but you want a certain level of swagger from someone making your sushi. There's a famous place called Sushi Yasuda in midtown, near Grand Central. About fifteen years ago, my father and I were eating there at the bar, and Chef Yasuda himself was serving us. My dad commented that he was quite impressed with the chef's knife, which was razor-sharp and almost comically large.

Yasuda responded with something I've never forgotten to this day: "Not the knife. The man handling the knife."

Truer words have never been spoken.

EPILOGUE
Final Thoughts

FOOD IS SUCH a huge part of who we are as people.

It's something that we all have in common—after all, everyone needs to eat! But it's also something that sets us apart and makes us unique. Every culture, every region, every city, and every family has their own culinary habits and traditions that define who they are.

Food can be a very personal and emotional thing, which is why I understand that this book may have made some people uncomfortable; maybe it's been jarring for me to talk about it from such a stark, money-focused, capitalistic viewpoint.

But the hospitality business, when done well, is the most beautiful, human-focused industry that has ever existed. If eating and drinking were only about sustenance, it wouldn't matter what we ate. We could just get our fill of calories and go on about our days. But meals are about so much more than that. They are our best opportunity to experience other lands or other cultures without leaving our own neighborhoods. The culinary arts give us a chance to see the world through a different set of lenses than we're used to.

There's something alluring and poetic about that to me, which is why I don't want to see people take it for granted, and allow unsavory characters and practices in the industry to ruin their experience.

I am a businessman. I want to make money. I want my employees to keep getting paid. I want my customers to keep their restaurants open. I want my producers to continue to catch fish. I want to see this entire industry continue to grow and thrive. But it has to be done carefully, thoughtfully, and with responsibility.

The past two years have been trying. The world survived an unprecedented crisis, one that disrupted every industry on the planet, none more so than my own. Yet we made it through.

What lessons will we take bring from that? I'm hoping that we all learned to take things a little slower, and to treat ourselves with a little bit more care. And part of that self-care should include more consciousness about what our bodies consume.

Food is too important to all of us to take chances on. It's not just your money that's at stake, but also your health, happiness, and well-being.

I wrote this book to be entertaining, but there was a serious purpose behind it. Everyone knows the saying "knowledge is power." That's not just an empty phrase. When people have a better understanding of what's going onto their plates, and into their bodies, that's a powerful thing. That's what I set out to do here—to correct the imbalance. To start to give power back to us, the people.

I know I've only just scratched the surface, but I hope I've made a little bit of progress toward that goal, and made you laugh a whole lot along the way.

Thank you for reading, and happy eating.

—Allen Ricca
November 2021

RECIPES

Dear Reader,

As we near the end of our literary journey, I would like to leave you with a little piece of my family. These are a collection of super easy and incredibly delicious recipes from my dad, Val. These are the dishes that my sister and I would beg our dad to make when we came home from college and needed a break from late-night pizza and chicken wings!

It was not uncommon for my mom and dad—both working parents—to have to come up with good meals, fast! And with one parent working in the seafood industry, we naturally always had varieties of seafood in the fridge and/or freezer. These shared recipes are designed so you do not have to hunt around for crazy ingredients at a variety of specialty stores. In fact, the only ingredient you should have to leave the house for, is the center of the plate: fish!

From street food and pizza to fancy dinners in Provence and Piedmont, I have done it all in terms of eating. I have enjoyed and treasured every culinary experience I have ever had, even the shitty ones, but these dishes and recipes I find to be truly special. As my dad has said hundreds of times, "These are your favorite chef's favorite dishes." There is something poetic in that, something beautiful and warming of the soul. These recipes are what you find your favorite chef chowing down on in the back of the kitchen after dinner service, usually with a great glass of wine and plenty of bread! So get yourself a good drink, put on some great music, and make these dishes with someone you love!

Thank you for taking the time to read this book.

All the love in the world,
Allen T. Ricca

Grilled Whole Fish, Mediterranean Style (serves 2)
What You Need:
- 2-2.5 lb. Whole fish of your choice (if cooking for 4 guests, simply use a 4 lb. fish)
- Salt
- Olive oil, Extra Virgin
- Juice of 1 lemon (Do not use bottled lemon juice)
- Pepper
- Oregano (any oregano will do)

For the Fish:
You will want to buy a 2 to 2.5 lb. whole fish. We recommend branzino, red snapper, or a black seabass. No matter the fish, you will want it scaled, gutted, gills removed, and fins trimmed. If you are experienced with this, more power to you, but we highly recommend having your local fish monger execute this task.

Method:
1. Pre-heat grill on high (ALL BURNERS).
2. Pat fish dry on both sides.
3. Lightly season the fish on both sides (pinch of salt per side).
4. After grill is heated for 5 minutes, scrub grill until it's *very* clean.
5. Use a cloth you do not need and dip in canola/vegetable oil and rub grill thoroughly (this creates a non-stick surface).
6. Place seasoned fish on grill horizontally, lowering heat to medium-high, closer to medium.

7. Close grill hood and allow fish to cook for 7 minutes. (If you are anxious and checking the fish by lifting cover of the grill, that is okay, but allow for maybe 2 extra minutes of cook time per side.)
8. Using a slotted fish spatula, carefully run along bottom of fish to release from grill and gently flip.
9. Once fish is flipped, allow to cook for 7 more minutes.
10. Carefully remove fish from grill and place on oval serving platter. Let rest.
11. In a small bowl add ¼ cup olive oil, the juice of 1 lemon, a pinch of salt, pepper, and oregano and whisk together.
12. Pour dressing over fish, fillet, and serve!

To fillet fish:

- Starting from the head of fish, take a knife and cut into meat along back bone (not more than ½-inch deep cut). Continue to work knife down to the tail, loosening meat from back bone.
- Using the knife, cut diagonally from top of head down toward belly, continuing to cut along belly to the tail.
- Now that the meat has been loosened from bone, take a large fork and starting from the head carefully remove fillet and place onto plate, leaving backbone exposed.
- With back bone exposed, starting from the tail, grab the back bone and gently lift all the way to the head until removed.
- You now have two completely edible and de-boned fillets! Grab a drink; you deserve it!

Linguini with White Clam Sauce (serves 4)

Cherrystone clams, unlike the littleneck clams for this recipe, will need to be shucked and clam juice preserved. If you do not know how to shuck clams, this is not a problem, as any seafood market or seafood counter can perform this task for you. Just ask them to preserve the clam juice!

What You Need:

- ¾ cup olive oil

- 1 entire head of garlic, peeled and crushed
- Pinch of crushed red pepper
- 3 pieces of anchovies
- 1 dozen Chopped cherrystone clams
- Clam juice from the shucked cherrystone clams
- 2 pinches of salt
- 1 lb. linguini
- Pinch of black pepper
- Pinch of dried oregano
- 2 dozen littleneck clams, scrubbed and cleaned
- 10 sprigs of parsley (leaf only)

Method:
1. Heat a large pan to medium/high heat and add olive oil, garlic, crushed red pepper, and anchovies and sauté for one minute.
2. Add in chopped cherrystone meat and clam juice and bring to a boil.
3. Once boiling, lower heat and allow to simmer.
4. Fill a separate pot with water, add salt, and bring to rapid boil.
5. When water is boiling, add linguini and allow to cook until al dente.
6. Once linguini is cooked, carefully strain pasta over sink and let sit (do not rinse pasta).
7. Meanwhile, turn heat on pan back to medium/high and add black pepper, oregano, and 2 dozen littleneck clams.
8. Cover pan with lid and allow clams to cook until open.
9. Once clams have opened, take your pasta in strainer and add back to empty pasta pot.
10. Take clam mixture and pour onto pasta, add parsley, and serve with bread.

Shrimp Cocktail (serves 3–4)
What You Need:
- 1 lb. of wild, headless, white shrimp (size U-12—12 Shrimp per 1 lb.)
- Ice bath (water with plenty of ice)

For the shrimp:

Of course you could use a pre-peeled and deveined shrimp, farmed or wild, but for this recipe Val likes using a U-12 Mexican wild white shrimp, headless and with the shell on. You can buy these at any seafood counter or seafood market. Following these steps will allow the shrimp to retain their moisture, giving a nice snap when you bite into them. The method outlined below will also reduce the shrimp's shrinkage and will keep the tails from over-curling.

Method:

1. Take your medium-sized pot and fill halfway with water.
2. With your steam insert already in the pot, boil water on high heat (this will help during the cooking process, as opposed to inserting post-water boiling).
3. Once the water has boiled, reduce heat to medium and line steam tray with shrimp with the shells still on (DO NOT OVERCROWD).
4. Let steam for 2 minutes and give them a stir.
5. Let cook for another 90 seconds.
6. After the final 90 seconds of steaming, carefully remove shrimp and place in ice bath (this will stop the cooking process).
7. After several minutes of cooling in the ice bath, it is now time to peel and devein the shrimp.
8. Remove the shells carefully, but at this point you are not going to hurt the shrimp, so rip those shells off!
9. Take a paring knife and lightly run it along the backside of the shrimp (top to tail), exposing the long vein. Remove vein as best you can and repeat procedure to the rest of the shrimp. You can choose to leave the tail on or remove during this process, but preference is to leave the tail on. You may find that leaving the tail on makes for a better presentation.
10. Serve with your favorite cocktail sauce, and voila!

Shrimp with Garlic *(Camarones ajillo)* (serves 4)

It's incredibly important to understand that the shrimp and olive oil are the stars here and water is their sworn enemy! Use a 26/30 size shrimp, preferably wild and preferably from Mexico, Texas, Florida—more importantly, *wild* shrimp. The point of emphasis on *wild* is that wild shrimp contain fewer chemicals than farmed shrimp. While not awful, farmed shrimp contain more chemicals/preservatives, which means more water seeps out during the cooking process, taking away from the flavor of the shrimp, olive oil, and garlic. Use the right shrimp, good olive oil, and plenty of garlic and you will not need parsley, paprika, lemon or anything else . . . just some good bread to mop up the sauce left behind!

What You Need:
- ¼ cup olive oil (Extra Virgin)
- Entire head of garlic (sliced paper thin)
- 1 lb. 26/30 size shrimp, peeled *but un-deveined* (leave vein in)
- Pinch of black pepper
- Pinch of salt

Method:
1. Start by heating your sauté pan over high heat for 3 to 4 minutes, at which point you will want to add ¼ cup of olive oil and all of the sliced garlic. Allow the garlic to sauté for about 30 seconds, bringing out the fragrance, but keeping a close eye to ensure garlic does not burn.
2. At this point it is time for the talent to make its way to the main stage! Add those shrimp to the sauté pan and allow them to become well acquainted with the other stars of this dish, the garlic and olive oil! Add your pinch of salt and black pepper and be sure to keep everything moving around (sautéing) over high heat for 4 to 5 minutes or until shrimp turn pink.

Shrimp with Lobster Sauce (serves 2 to 4 people)
What You Need:
- 2 tablespoons peanut, canola, or vegetable oil
- 2 tablespoons finely chopped garlic
- 1 lb. shrimp, size 21/25, peeled and deveined
- ½ tablespoon of finely chopped ginger
- ¼ lb. ground pork
- 4 pieces of scallion, chopped (separate the green from the white portion of scallion)
- 1 cup chicken broth
- 1 pinch of salt
- 1 pinch of pepper
- 1 tablespoon cornstarch dissolved in 2 oz. of water
- 1 egg

Method:
1. Using a deep frying pan, heat over high.
2. Add half the oil and half the garlic (1 tablespoon of each) and *all* the shrimp.
3. Sauté shrimp for 45 seconds to 1 minute.
4. Pour contents of pan onto plate and set off to the side.
5. Put pan back on high heat and add remaining oil, garlic, all of the ginger, all of the ground pork, and white portion of chopped scallion.
6. With all ingredients in pan, sauté pork until separated and evenly distributed.
7. Add 1 cup chicken broth and bring to a boil.
8. Add pinch of salt and pinch of pepper.
9. Add back shrimp to pan and cook for 1 minute.
10. Add 1 tablespoon of cornstarch dissolved in water.
11. Stir for 30 seconds until contents begin to thicken.
12. Turn off heat, crack egg, and stir into mixture.
13. Immediately add the remaining green scallion and serve over white rice.*

*This is a dish that is traditionally served over white rice, but feel free to sub brown rice or use no rice at all! Either way, you cannot go wrong, as it is absolutely delicious.

The Best Baked Clams (serves 4 to 6)
What You Need:
- 2 dozen clams (top necks or littlenecks)
- 2 cloves of fresh garlic, finely chopped
- 3 tablespoons of parsley, finely chopped
- 1 cup of plain or pre-seasoned breadcrumb
- Olive oil
- Water

For the Clams:
Choose a clam that is in line with what you are comfortable with. If you like a bigger/meatier clam, use a Top Neck, but for this recipe Val likes using Littlenecks. Buy clams that are closest to your geographic territory. If you are in Vermont, *do not* use a clam from Virginia or Florida. Ask your seafood monger and they will surely point you in the right direction, especially by asking key questions and using correct language.

For the breading mixture:
In a bowl, combine garlic, parsley, breadcrumbs, and 1 tablespoon of olive oil.

Method:
1. Preheat oven to 425 degrees.
2. Rinse the clams and give a light rub to get sand off.
3. Carefully and safely open your clams by using a proper clam knife, removing muscle on top and bottom of clam.
4. On baking tray, arrange clams so they are not overcrowding.
5. Place some of the breading mixture on top of each clam, allowing overflow onto tray.
6. After mixture is on clams, place 1 teaspoon of water on top of mixture.
7. After mixture and water are added to each clam, go back and add another, much thinner layer of mixture, careful not to overflow this time (think a dusting).

8. Add a half-teaspoon/very light drizzle of olive oil to each clam.
9. Add just enough water to tray to lightly coat bottom, then place in pre-heated oven and allow to bake for roughly 8 minutes or until golden brown. (Cooking time may vary depending on size of clams, so monitor until golden brown.)

Zuppa De Clams, also known as Clams in Red Sauce (serves 4)
What you need:
- 2 tablespoons of Extra Virgin Olive Oil
- Whole head of garlic (sliced thin)
- 3 anchovies
- 1 teaspoon of crushed red pepper
- 1 large can whole San Marzano Tomatoes, sliced (less the liquid)
- 1 teaspoon of black pepper
- 3 dozen top neck clams, rinsed and scrubbed clean
- Entire loaf of bread

Method:
1. Heat a large sauté pan over medium to high heat and add olive oil.
2. After a few minutes of heating oil in pan, add your entire head of garlic, anchovies, and red pepper.
3. Allow to sauté for 30 seconds making sure not to burn garlic.
4. Add in sliced San Marzano tomatoes only—no liquid from can.
5. Add black pepper, cover pan, and reduce heat to low and allow to simmer for 15 minutes.
6. After 15 minutes of simmering, raise heat to medium/high, add clams, and cover pan.

---

*The key to recipe is water and second thin layer of mixture with olive oil. It adds a level of depth and flavor while giving a nice golden brown crust to your clam. As we allowed first layer to overflow off the clam, that excess mixture combined with the liquid during cooking process will make you and your bread very happy once you get to dipping!

7. Allow clams to cook until opened, roughly 8-10 minutes.
8. Serve in large serving bowl with loaf of bread!

*This recipe also doubles as Shrimp Marinara. Instead of using clams, simply use 1 lb. of U/15 size shrimp, fully cleaned (no shells or veins, tail on/off—chef's choice)! Follow all steps the same, except for one caveat—when adding the cleaned shrimp, only allow to cook for 3 minutes. Voila—two for the price of one!

APPENDIX
Quick Guide to Buying Seafood and Fish

WHEN BUYING SEAFOOD at a store, one can easily get hung up trying to gauge how much to buy. Even at a restaurant it can be tricky—how much is enough? Is the whole fish too big to order for one, can I maybe convince my date to share this with me? How many "jumbo" shrimp do I buy at the grocery store to feed two people? How many for four?! These things can be plaguing and while we are all different in size and appetites I think I can provide some pro-tips to help ease the pain and make good quick decisions.

Sizing of seafood such as scallops and shrimp should never be presented as jumbo, large, medium, or small. Shrimp and scallop size is represented by a number range that dictates how many physical pieces will make up one pound. When you know how many pieces make up one pound, you can easily navigate the supermarket and make proper decisions when purchasing ingredients.

> *A large size* of scallop would be a U-10/Under 10 pieces of scallops to 1 lb.
>> Center of plate entrée-size scallop
>>> A hungrier adult can easily eat 6/7 U-10 scallops
>>> A less hungry adult can easily eat 5 U-10 scallops

A smaller size scallop would be a 10-20/10-20 scallops per 1 lb.
   Appetizer-size scallop or served in a pasta or salad
       A hungrier adult can eat 9 or 10 scallops (appetizer by itself)
       A less hungry adult can eat 6 or 7 scallops (appetizer by itself)
       If serving with pasta or a salad, 5 scallops for either partner

An even smaller size of scallop would be a 20–30 scallop/20–30 scallops per 1 lb.
   Stir-fry size scallop or perfect in wraps due to their "bite sizeness"
       If other proteins in your stir-fry, maybe sprinkle in 10 scallops
       If making a wrap, depending on contents, no more than 5 or 6

A large shrimp U-8, U-10, or U-12/Under 8, 10, or 12 pieces of shrimp per 1lb.
   Shrimp Cocktail, Grilled Shrimp, Skewered Shrimp, and Fried Shrimp
       Average adults will consume 3 or 4 shrimp cocktail
       A hungrier adult will eat 6 or 7 grilled or fried shrimp
       A less hungry adult will eat 4 or 5 grilled or fried shrimp

A smaller size shrimp, U/15; 16/20; 21/25 (most common size Chinese cuisine)
   Pasta, Noodles, Rice, or even over a Salad
       Avg. adults can consume 5 to 6 shrimp each in a starch based dish
       Avg. adults can consume 6 to 7 shrimp each in a salad, if entrée
       Avg. adults can consume 4 to 5 shrimp each in a salad, if appetizer

An even smaller size shrimp 26/30; 31/40; 41/50 (head to frozen food aisle)
   Tacos, wraps, sandwiches, and soups

You do not need a seafood monger—just grab in frozen food aisle

For a family of four you will want 2 lbs. of any size

These sizes come packed in 2 lb. bags—cleaned and ready to go

*Shrimp can keep getting smaller and smaller, but what you have here is a good cheat sheet. This won't solve all your problems, but will most certainly take A LOT of the guess work out of your next trip to shop for your shrimp.

Let's talk fish . . .

I can eat steak all day long, which drives my wife insane, but hey, I am a true American when it comes to my love of red meat and I do not apologize for it! Protein is protein is protein, so when we are discussing how much fish to order or purchase I find it is helpful to think in terms of what you are most familiar with and most Americans are familiar with red meat. An average burger is an eight-ounce patty and that is going to come with some tomato, lettuce, onion, and pickles and of course a bun, but the protein is eight ounces, so that is your benchmark. A normal New York strip is anywhere from twelve to sixteen ounces, and I think most people can picture seeing that on a menu or in a display case at a butcher or grocery store. So fish portions and fillets are no different!

Fillets and portions of your preferred fish for an entree
Hungry adults can easily consume a 10-12 oz. fillet of fish
Less hungry adults can easily consume 8-10 oz. fillet of fish
Child size portion is around a 6 oz. fillet
For a family of four you would want 2 lbs of your favorite fish, filleted
Fillets and portions over salad or stuffed
Fish over a salad should call for 6 oz. of fish
If being forced to eat lettuce and hungrier than avg. use 8 oz. of fish
If stuffing a fillet with say crabmeat you may want to use an 6-8 oz. fillet

For stuffing try using a mild white flakey fish, like flounder

Whole Fish Bronzino, Red snapper, and Black sea bass

An avg. person should have no trouble consuming a 1–1.25 lb fish

A hungrier than avg. person will want a 1.5 lb. fish

An avg. couple sharing a whole fish will want to split a 2–3 lb. fish

A hungrier than avg. couple will want a 3–4 lb. whole fish

Sandwiches and Taco Tuesday

Use cod, flounder, or grouper (blackened, fried, or grilled) for a sammie

Cut or have them cut into into 3–4 oz. portions

A hungry person can easily eat 4 tacos

A less hungry person (like my wife) can eat 2 tacos

A family of four should plan for 8 tacos and purchase 1.75–2 lbs. of fish

Pro-Tip for convenience: seek out already portioned fish in your frozen food aisle. Frozen fish portions are incredibly easy and allow you to thaw just what you need and put rest away for another meal.

Don't be intimidated at the grocery store. You now have knowledge— use it!

ACKNOWLEDGMENTS

ACKNOWLEDGMENTS ARE TRICKY. You want to make sure you do not leave anyone off, but at the same time you must acknowledge the fact that you are inevitably forgetting someone and it will come back to kick you in the butt at some point. Whether it be a cocktail party or a business setting, they will passive-aggressively call you out and make five minutes or so quite awkward while you squirm for an excuse! That being said, let's acknowledge some people who had quite a bit to do with making this book something that I'm immensely proud of.

First and foremost, I want to thank my family. Mom and Dad, thank you for being who you are and giving Emily and me the childhood we had, joyfully raising us around music, food, and exposing us to as much culture as you could. Dad, I miss having you at the office and I thank you for giving me the freedom to run and grow your company. Mom, what can I say? You have always believed that I can do anything and have always been my number-one fan. Given your background as a career educator and teacher of the English language, I hope this writing makes you proud and that you're able to read it on a nice beach somewhere.

To my fabulous agent Sharon Bowers, who never once gave up on me and always believed in this project from the second we met. I'll never forget that day at your midtown Manhattan office when we shared a coffee and you patiently listened to me stammer over my words as I pitched this book. Thank you also for not raising an eyebrow when I unceremoniously dumped about two hundred pages of notes on your desk.

This book is not a book without Joe Muto. My co-writer and friend, you are as good a person as there is to work with. I thank you more than you'll ever know for sharing my brain and translating my thoughts as naturally as you do. Honestly, it's sort of scary! You never lost steam on this project or me and were always patient even when I'd pester you at all hours of the day and night. You are a great father and husband, a loyal friend, and I appreciate you writing this book with me; I know your parents Tony and Joanie will be proud.

This book does not exist without our fabulous editor Julie Ganz. Thank you for your kindness, and your diligent handholding as we went through this process. You took a big chance on me, and I'll be forever grateful for the faith that you put into this novice author. Thank you for a smooth, efficient editing process that felt like a truly collaborative relationship. I never once felt anything other than pure happiness working with you. Thank you for giving me the opportunity to learn about a whole different industry, and being so generous with your time to talk me through matters big and small. Your little boy is quite lucky to have such a cool mom!

To everyone I work with, directly and indirectly: This story can only be told thanks to the massive team that works hard and professionally, every single day. To all my employees at all our companies—this is for us. You guys wake up every single day and allow me to lead you. It is an honor and a privilege to work side-by-side with you all, and to feel so much energy and loyalty from you.

Thank you to Dominic, who has worked for my dad since I was knee-high, and would babysit me and take me to Knicks games and feed me Ranch One Chicken. To Chris, who was my dad's first employee: thank you for holding my hand and taking me to get lunch as we walked through Bed-Stuy in the early nineties. To Bob, who has been as loyal a guy as has ever existed for his entire career, thank you for working so easily with me and helping me find success. To Philip, you started your career working alongside my dad and I am so honored you'll finish your career at his son's side. Your patience with me has been endless, and your wife Jade's cooking is pure bliss! To Dino, if it were not for you and your ability to lead, I would never have been able to branch out and purchase other companies, never been able to run them the way I needed to, and never been able to write this book. The freedom you provide me through your sheer dedication and hard work is something I cannot truly articulate, as there are not enough words to express my thanks. To Joey and Shelby, I look so very forward to the wedding! I remain in constant awe of how quickly you learn, and your eagerness to take on new tasks every single day without question or fear. To my brother-in-law Will, I am happy to have such a fun, beer-loving, hard-working friend and colleague that I get to see day in and day out. I hope we continue to build something special for Annabelle and Eloise!

To Willis Rivkin, my business partner at Winchell Mountain Coffee, thank you for your continued dedication to roasting the finest beans in the world. Working with you over the years has been special—we have certainly come a long way since fifteen years old, huh? To my dear friend and business associate Sandra Boynton, you continue to make me laugh and force me to think differently when it comes to business. I look forward to our early morning calls, French lessons, and all our fun work together. To Mike, Chris, Michele, Peter, Maureen, and Mike Guinard, thank you for listening to me and taking to my leadership style in the wine industry even though I did not know anything about wine!

Lastly, I want to thank all of the stewards of culture in the Food & Beverage industry. The hospitality industry is a demanding and difficult field to work in even during good times, and these fine people have been whacked upside the head with a two-by-four these past couple years. We as a community need to rally behind these hardworking folks, and make sure we help rebuild an important part of this country: the shared culture that comes through food. Restaurants and the dining industry are not just important for purposes of enjoying a night out—it goes much deeper than that. These are establishments that allow you to go to Ethiopia or Japan without even leaving your own neighborhood! We get to learn more about a culture that is halfway around the world, right in our own backyards. We must never lose sight of this, as food is a common denominator for all people.

To anyone I might be leaving off, sorry and I'll catch you on the flip side!

—Allen Ricca

I'm indebted to my lovely wife Jenny, my son Max, and my dog Linus, who put up with all the weird hours and tight deadlines that come with getting any book over the finish line.

I'm further indebted to my in-laws in Pittsburgh and my parents in Cincinnati, both of whom I stayed with several times over the course of the COVID-disrupted summer of 2021, when the bulk of this book was written.

I'd like to reiterate Allen's thanks to Sharon, who never lost faith at any point over the long process of bringing this book to fruition; and to Julie, who saw the potential of the project and provided us with thoughtful, intelligent edits that only made the book more concise and focused.

Above all, I'd like to thank Allen for bringing me in on this. I've known him for a long time, and I can truly say that I've never met any-one like him. He's a force of nature, with a work ethic so energetic that it took me—a classic procrastinator—literal months to catch up to him.

All of the thoughts, opinions, and anecdotes in this book are his. Most of the words are, too. My purpose here was simply to help orga-nize and clarify the voluminous first draft that he cranked out in record time. I appreciate him putting his trust in me, and hope that I've main-tained his uniquely entertaining voice, and done justice to this topic that he has an encyclopedic knowledge of.

He's an incredible creative partner, and an even better friend, and it's been a thrill to help him bring this passion project to life.

—Joe Muto